The S[illegible]ss:
Evang[illegible] Today

Edited by Wendy S. Robins and
Gillian Hawney

The United Society for the Propagation of the Gospel
Partnership House
157 Waterloo Road
London
SE1 8XA

First published 1992

Partnership House
157 Waterloo Road
London
SE1 8XA

ISBN 0 85472 035 9

CIP data applied for

USPG/756/3m/July 1992

Photoset and printed by Stanley L. Hunt (Printers) Ltd
Midland Road
Rushden
Northamptonshire

Contents

Introduction

How should we in Britain respond to the call for a 'Decade of Evangelism'? What can we learn from the church in other parts of the world as we seek to answer this question?

What is evangelism? What is mission? What is God's activity in the late twentieth century, and how does that activity make itself visible in a world full of struggle, pain and oppression?

USPG asked people from around the world church to reflect upon these questions and the results of their reflections are offered here.

In the many different places around the world where the authors live and work God can be seen to work in different ways and through different structures. What is crucial is that wherever God's people are they should be enabled to perceive God through the whole of life and begin to share these insights with others. If this begins to happen then the work of the Decade of Evangelism will result in us taking on new patterns and models.

It is hoped that the essays contained in *The scandal of the cross* will enable those engaged in God's mission to gain new ways of discerning God's action and to learn from the vision of those elsewhere in the world.

Each of the essays brings a uniqueness of geographical and cultural perspective, and a difference in style and rhythm. Some essays communicate largely through story and example while others begin from a more traditional theological view. All the contributions however look for ways of breaking out of the old Western patterns that sometimes trap us.

From wherever they come and in whatever context they live our writers offer to all those who read this material a freshness which will give an enlarged vision to all who want to take God's mission seriously, particularly in this Decade of Evangelism.

Wendy S. Robins
July 1992

Jesus and Mission: Some Redefinitions

R. S. Sugirtharajah

Among other things, the mention of the Decade of Evangelism brings to mind 'conversion', 'revival' and 'sharing'. These words have a long association with the Christian churches' missionary enterprise and they evoke mixed feelings. In popular understanding they have come to mean the following: bringing people of other faiths to a belief in Christ as expressed by one of the many Christian denominations (conversion); emphasizing the spiritual and transcendental nature of Christian faith amid the onslaught from secular and other threats (revival); and spreading the Christian Good News to people who haven't heard the name of Jesus (sharing). Until now the Christian churches have had a clear understanding of what they have meant by these terms.

As they say in feminist circles, however, things have changed. The people of other faiths are no longer willing to be the passive recipients of a Christian missionary offensive. They too, believe that they have a message which is worth proclaiming. Besides this, there are two other pressing problems. They are:

- the increasing threat to the environment;
- the widening disparity between those who are economically advantaged and those who are underprivileged.

In the light of these changed circumstances, the church has to re-think and re-define the three terms. This article, drawing on the Jesus tradition, seeks to re-define these terms in order to meet the new contextual needs.

Conversion = Reorientation

Since the advent of the missionary era, the Christian church has been propagating Christianity among the members of other faiths. This swap is presented as a spiritual bonanza for these people. The assumption of the Christian church was that it was only other people who needed conversion.

But, in a religiously pluralistic context, where the Christian community is one among many, it is the church that needs conversion and a new understanding of God as one who cares for all people. In other words, conversion in our time is the Christian church reorienting itself from its tribal identity and chauvinistic theological attitudes and acknowledging God's compassion and mercy for all.

Evangelizing the evangelizer

An incident that highlights the need for reorientation is Jesus' encounter with the Canaanite woman (Matt. 15.21-28. Mark 7.24-30). Traditionally, this episode has been understood mainly from a Christian triumphalistic point of view and seen as Jesus rendering a great service to a Gentile woman by alleviating her pain. What this overly mission-oriented and church-centred reading often overlooks is that this ministration is reciprocal. Not only was the Canaanite woman helped, but she in her turn helped Jesus. She did a great service to him by enabling him to broaden his particularistic and intolerant understanding of non-Jews, an understanding which separated and segregated Gentiles as unclean and impure. Bultmann, in his comments on this narrative, notes that on this occasion Jesus was not the victor. In his view, the main aspect of this episode is not the healing but 'the change in Jesus' behaviour as the dialogue goes on'.[1] This change in Jesus can be easily seen as the conversation between Jesus and the woman unfolds.

According to Matthew, Jesus, a Galilean Jew, and an unnamed Canaanite woman are drawn together because of a specific human need. Unlike Mark, who identifies this woman in national and political categories (a Greek from the region of Syrian Phoenicia), Matthew highlights her religious affiliation and calls her a Canaanite. The Jewish opposition to the religion of the Canaanites is well documented in their scriptural texts. Moreover 'Canaanite' is an expression frequently used in the Hebrew scriptures to describe those who are not part of the elect people of God. When she approached Jesus to ask him to help her daughter, his reply echoed two things; the special priority of his own people, and their racial purity. In the first part of the reply – 'I was sent only to the lost sheep of the house of Israel' – Jesus was not only reiterating the ethnic, cultural and socio-political prejudices that existed in his day between Jews and Gentiles, but was also envisioning his task as restoring the status of Jews as God's special people. He was restating the first-century popular Israelite perception. This was a common prejudice of that time. For example, we see the same narrow theological assumption in Paul. He exhibits and exudes national pride in his disputes with Gentile Christians (Rom. 1.16, 2.9-10, 3.1-2).

The second part of Jesus' reply, 'It is not fair to take the children's bread and throw it to the dogs', further reinforces the idea of the racial purity of the

Jews by figuratively alluding to the Gentiles as dogs. This reply may raise a few eyebrows among those who take the Race Relations Act seriously. But what is intriguing about this harsh response is that in the preceding episode (Matt. 15.1-20. Mark 7.1-23) Jesus had severely criticised the beliefs about pollution and purity that were practised among his own community and by the Pharisees on the basis of external ritual. Basing his perspective on the Hebrew scripture, Jesus confronted the Pharisees and challenged the Pharisaic understanding of purity which segregated people and created boundaries within their own community. Jesus not only advocated the breaking down of these boundaries, but also put it into practice by entering into social contact with his community's forbidden and unclean people – the lost sheep of the house of Israel – women, tax-collectors, lepers, children and eunuchs.

Jesus is challenged

In his interaction with this Gentile woman however, we see Jesus working within the theological framework of his day, and his failure to transcend this narrow view. His complacent outlook gets a rude shock when the woman replies sharply, 'Yes, lord, yet even the dogs eat the crumbs that fall from their master's table'. The reference to table-sharing in the woman's reply must have shaken Jesus. In her sharp response she was trying to remind Jesus that God's hospitality is abundant enough to go beyond national and racial boundaries.

It was this astute theological reply that enabled Jesus to liberate himself from the prevailing Jewish theology and contemporary reading of the Hebrew scriptures concerning the Gentiles. It leads to an active openness and acceptance of people who were excluded by the Judaism(s) of his day. His response to her and his actions in the subsequent narratives bear this out. In other words, it is the evangelizer who is evangelized now. Sharon Ringe sees this as 'the woman's ministry *to* [italics hers] Jesus by her 'faith' – a faith that is no doctrinal confession of his messianic identity, and no flattery of his apparently miraculous powers, but rather an act of trust, of engagement, and risking everything.'[2] This new openness is not only reflected in his reply, 'O Woman, great is your faith! Be it done for you as you desire', but also enables Jesus to heal and respond and act as a vehicle of God's gratuitous love, compassion and hospitality.

What follows after this episode is indicative of Jesus' change of heart and new attitude. Matthew and Mark describe a similar sequence of events. The Canaanite woman does not follow Jesus. She vanishes from the scene. But it is Jesus who journeys into Gentile territory and makes God's compassion available by healing (Matt. 15.29-31), and by breaking the table taboo by giving sustenance to four thousand Gentiles who had nothing to eat (Matt.

15.32-39). Jesus' feeding of the Gentiles was indicative of two things: firstly, God's compassion was abundant enough not only to encompass the Jews but also the Gentiles, and, secondly, God is open enough to accept doubly-polluted Gentiles. It is after this sojourn in the Gentile region and being with the non-Jews that Jesus starts to re-assess his role and his task. This is remarkably evident in the next chapter, when he poses the question to his own circle of friends and tries to evaluate his function as God's messenger.

Conversion within a tradition

What the Canaanite episode indicates is that conversion can take place within a religious tradition itself and it does not necessarily mean changing from one religious tradition to another. It can mean reorienting to a new dimension of one's own faith. Jesus' encounter with the Canaanite woman enabled him to widen his understanding of God and his attitude to people who were not part of his own community. Instead of converting others, the Christian church should, like Jesus, reorient itself to the availability of God's grace outside its own circles. It should recognize that the channels of grace are available to everyone and should not insist that it has the monopoly. In the Decade of Evangelism, it is the Christian church which must be converted. It must gain new eyes to recognize God's presence outside its compound; gain new ears to hear God's voice beyond its pulpit; gain new hands to stretch out wherever God's liberative and healing action go on; and gain new feet to walk beyond the church building to discover a new dimension of God.

Revival = Revitalizing

In some Christian circles revival is understood in terms of inner spiritual renewal, purity of heart and the well-being of the individual. Though these are valid and play an important role, Christians need to re-think revival not so much as accentuating the spiritual value of the individual but as revitalizing the Christian tradition by recovering some of its forgotten aspects in order to face pressing new questions such as the threat to the environment and ecological destruction.

Increasingly in scholarly circles, Jesus is coming to be seen as a person who revitalized his own tradition. While his contemporaries were trying to propagate one aspect of the Jewish God as pure and holy, Jesus, through his teaching and actions, was trying to announce a long-overlooked facet of the Jewish God – God as the compassionate one. Jesus' disagreement with his contemporaries was not about the adequacy of Judaism, but about how one interprets the Torah – whether it has to be interpreted from the perspective of holiness or from the perspective of compassion.

The notion of God as holy was the dominant theme at the time when Jesus was engaged in his public activity. This had emerged as an interpretative strategy during the exile and continued to dominate Jewish thinking till the time of Jesus. Holiness was seen as a system of defining and discriminating people and objects. The influential group of the day, the Pharisees, took seriously the obligation laid upon Israel to be a holy nation before God, 'You shall be holy; for I the Lord your God am Holy' (Lev. 19.2, 11.44). They extended the concern for cultic purity beyond the temple and applied it to all aspects of life. Their propagation of a holy and righteous God resulted in the separation and isolation of the community. For Jesus, holiness meant reaching out and accepting people, not segregating them and erecting boundaries. Jesus, as the initiator of a revitalizing movement within Judaism, opened up a fresh aspect of the God of Israel – God as merciful. Appealing to his own scriptural tradition, he was simply reiterating a forgotten aspect of God – as gracious and merciful (Ex. 34.6), and as a consequence he was urging his contemporaries to show solidarity and compassion towards one another. 'Be merciful, even as your Father is merciful' (Luke 6.36).

Jesus did not declare a new quality of God nor did he disclose new truth about God. Rather he recovered forgotten aspects of the Jewish concept of God in order to revitalize the tradition. He gave fresh life to overlooked aspects of the Jewish concept of God – God as merciful, compassionate and generous. In doing so, he was trying to give a fresh impetus and purpose to the Judaism(s) of his day which were alienating people. Jesus was not trying to invent something out of his imagination. Rather, he was trying to recover and revive a truth that was peripheralized by the religious interpreters of his time.

Revitalizing Christianity

Just as Jesus helped to revitalize his tradition, the Decade of Evangelism may be the appropriate time to revitalize the Christian faith by recovering some of its obscured biblical perspectives, in order to face one of the many serious crises that threaten our planet in this very decade – the exploitation and destruction of the environment. The Christian attitude towards the earth has been largely negative. This has been due to two factors:

- Christians have tended to appeal to a strand of biblical teaching which has encouraged alienation from the natural world. The Bible's emphasis on a transcendent and personal God has diminished our sense of divinity in nature. We have stressed the importance of individual human redemption and paid little attention to nature and creation as a whole. We have over-emphasized the spiritual nature of humans against the physical nature of the whole created order. The Fall was seen as a sufficient reason for creation's corruption and the need for domination. We have uncritically assumed the role of stewardship and subdued and subordinated the earth. This may be the time to bring back compassion for the earth and take care of the created order in humility.

- The Christian tendency to accord preferential treatment to the sacred historical events of the Bible as the means for discerning God's manifestation, has also affected our attitude towards the earth. The major historical events such as the Exodus, the Covenant and the Incarnation have been seen as the vehicles of God's self-disclosure. Thus, the experience of God through the realm of nature and the ordinary symbols of the environment have been under-interpreted and marginalized by the mainline theologies. This has not only led to a neglect of the earth but also to a failure to recognize natural revelation as legitimate data for theological enquiry.

Christians need to recover scriptural teachings which revere the created order. The Wisdom literature provides some interesting perspectives on creation, and offers correctives to the past imbalance in scriptural emphases. The sages celebrate and glorify the created order. The Wisdom affirmation is that God not only created the world but also arranged it in such a way that its various components neatly interconnect (Si. 16.26-28). The sages make us aware that the world is God's good creation and it is the place where we live and strive to achieve our goal. Jesus posits a deity who takes care of the ravens, the lilies and the sparrows. Paul's end-time vision is that humankind's salvation is inextricably linked with the liberation and transformation of the created order (Rom. 8). Thus in the Decade of Evangelism, revival has to be thought of in terms of revitalizing the Christian tradition in order to address the pressing ecological problems of our time. It means reclaiming and retrieving a biblical truth which has been marginalized by theological discourses down the centuries.

Sharing = Distribution

'Sharing' in popular Christian parlance means proclaiming the saving act of Jesus. This sharing is mainly verbal. In the Decade of Evangelism what we need to share with people is not only the Good News but also the goods. It means redistributing the world's resources among people who lack the necessities of life.

An example of such sharing is the feeding miracle recorded in the synoptic gospels. The standard Euro-American interpretation is determined by the fact that the exegete is talking to secularized, middle-class people who have serious objections to such texts and cannot accept the supernatural element in the episode. The clue to the text is seen in the dialogue between Jesus and his disciples. While Jesus wanted to feed the people, the disciples thought only in terms of buying food. They tried to tell Jesus to send the people away so that they could 'buy themselves something to eat' (Mark 6.37). They had also worked out the cost as around 200 denarius. Jesus' reply was, 'How many loaves have you? Go and see'. What this conversation highlights is that the disciples and Jesus represent two types of economy. One based on the market and governed by market forces and the power of money, and the other based on a system that promotes gift giving and the sharing of resources. What the narrative advocates is the promotion of a gift-relationship, whereby everything belongs to everyone. The narrative is not about a miracle or whether it is scientifically possible to multiply food. There is nothing supernatural about it. The only miracle here is the triumph of an economics of sharing resources within a community over an economy of buying and money power. It is about redistributing available resources within the community.[3]

Sharing resources today

A number of studies commissioned by church and secular agencies have shown that people both in the South and in the North are deprived of the basic necessities of life. They lack these essential needs not because they are not available or because there is not sufficient to go around. They lack these fundamental amenities because resources are unevenly distributed. This imbalance is the direct consequence of a market economy which enables a few to hog and accumulate at the expense of the many. The basic needs of many people will not be met until the present unequal distribution of resources is rectified. The Pentecostal community in Jerusalem was characterized by the community of goods (Acts 2.44-45). This community held everything in common, and distributed goods among the destitute. The result of such an arrangement according to Luke was that there were no needy among them. Sharing in this Decade of Evangelism means the Christian church ensuring that resources are made available to all people, and bridging the gap between those who have more than they need and those who do not have enough.

A final thought

Some time ago, Canon Max Warren, commenting on traditional mission policy and practice wrote: 'We have marched around the alien Jerichos the requisite number of times. We have sounded the trumpets and the walls have not collapsed.' An apocryphal story from India may provide the clue for this apparent failure. About a hundred years ago, the brahmin priests were alarmed to hear of the visit of a very important Anglican church dignitary to India. They thought that this foreign religion might become a threat to their own tradition so they sent one of their men to assess the situation. As he stood at the bishop's mansion, he saw the great man walk down the steps arrayed in magnificent robes and go off in a gorgeous horse-drawn carriage. The spy returned to his friends. 'Have no fear', he said, 'this is not a religion we need to fear.' The priests were relieved. Moral: the pomp and splendour of the organized church hold no appeal for genuine seekers after truth.

The trouble with any coordinated evangelism, be it traditional preaching, or engagement in development work, is that it is likely to give the wrong signal to outsiders. Too often it gives the impression of the Christian church displaying its organizational power and flexing its institutional muscles. Organized evangelism, whatever form it takes, runs the risk of not witnessing to God's love but of demonstrating the institutional might and the financial power of the church. The church's intention may be authentic but to the outside world it does not convey God's solidarity with the people. Any orchestrated mission activity, whether evangelism or development work, will reinforce the notion that the church is a tribal body serving the tribal and vested interest of Christians. What the Christian church needs to do in this Decade of Evangelism is to demonstrate its vulnerability. The synoptic gospels contain instructions for travelling missioners. They provide a catalogue of things which missioners are proscribed from taking with them. They include money, bag, staff, sandals, food and extra clothing. All these prohibitions point to the helplessness and vulnerability of the missioners. Going without money is a sign of trust. Lack of a staff signifies defencelessness. Without the begging bowl, one is dependent entirely on others for food. Going barefoot is a sign of poverty. These sanctions may be out of place in the present urbanized world. But what they indicate is the image of the missioner being truly without resources and protection. Today the Christian church has enough gold and silver. That is why it is difficult for the church to say, as Peter did: 'rise up and walk'. What these prohibitions demonstrate is the powerlessness of the missioner. It is this powerlessness that the church is called upon to embody in the Decade of Evangelism.

Notes

1 R. Bultmann, *The history of the synoptic tradition* (Basil Blackwell, Oxford, 1963).
2 S. H. Ringe, 'A gentile woman's story', in *Feminist interpretations of the Bible,* edited by L. Russell (Basil Blackwell, Oxford, 1985).
3 C. Meyers, *Binding the strong man: A political reading of Mark's story of Jesus* (Orbis Books, New York, 1988).

Sainthood and Evangelism

Musimbi Kanyoro

Sainthood

On November 2nd the English-speaking congregation of the Lutheran Church in Geneva joined the rest of the Christian world in celebrating All Saints Day. The pastor of the church asked the congregation to think of someone, alive or dead, who had had an influence on their Christian faith. We were asked to bring to church pictures or other artifacts through which our memories of these people, 'the saints in our lives', were evoked. We were also given the freedom to just think about them or write something on paper that helped us remember them in a special way.

I remember hearing this announcement and feeling lost. Who had made an impact on my Christian journey of faith? What did she/he do? When? Where? Was it one person or many? It was so much easier for me to think of my mother and other members of my family who had had the direct responsibility for my upbringing. And I did think of them. I could also quite easily come up with a reasonable number of artifacts, such as photos, personal possessions or gifts from them, as for example my grandfather's Bible, my mother-in-law's 'kiondo basket', and the several items of clothing my mother had made for my family. But the more I thought about the 'saints' in my life, the more I became convinced that it was a new issue for me. I had not sufficiently reflected on it. My Christian faith had grown from stage to stage and I had simply continued to travel on this journey with so many others. Sometimes I had been taken by the hand, as in the early childhood care of me by my parents and Sunday school teachers; other times I had been safely in the company of Christian communities at school, university and at church.

Later the same week I read 'Newsweek'[1] which carried an article on 'The making of saints'. This led me to go to the library and to explore more about sainthood. Learning about the issues involved in the church's canonization of saints, taught me that if ever there were saints in my life they will never be known, let alone canonized by the church, and therefore I do well to take the time to name them. It is up to me to remember them, to write about them and to canonize them in my heart. These saints, for me, are the many women and men who understand the message of the gospel as serving one another; dying with each other, and even dying for one another. Through their lives, others came to have glimpses of God and God's kingdom. Through their actions, the gospel is heard even by those who cannot read it for themselves and Christ's message becomes alive and relevant. Through their testimonies Jesus' words became flesh. I have sometimes heard or read about these saints. I have also at other times had occasion to be among them, without even being aware of it. Yet, they have affected my life. They have challenged me to repent and to be grateful for the gift of Jesus Christ.

I remember one such occasion. I was about fifteen years old, a teenager going through my inquisitive period. My mother was ill. She could not go to her women's 'ushirika' group and asked me to go in her place. On that day, the group was going to help 'Mama Berita'. Mama Berita had gone through many sad moments. Her two-year-old child had died of malaria, and she had had a miscarriage and as a consequence was very unhappy and ill. Her 'shamba' (farm) had been unattended and her house needed some repairs. Mama Berita was not strong enough even to cook for the rest of her family who still depended on her. So the women's ushirika group had come to help her out. I was excited to go on behalf of my ill mother, partly out of curiosity. My mother always gave these ushirika working groups a high priority on her calendar. I was curious and wanted to know what this group was all about.

When I arrived to join the group all the women seemed happy to welcome me. Although I was only a youth among them I felt comfortable and was happy in this group of my 'mothers', for in my culture all of them are my mothers and I am their daughter. We are expected by culture to accept the responsibilities involved in the daughter-mother, mother-daughter relationship by being members of the same community.

The day's task was to work on the farm, weeding the maize and planting vegetables. I must confess that I did not at all fancy digging and was afraid that my performance would fall short of that of the others. As soon as we started my fears were erased. For these women worked not as individuals but as a group. They seemed to shelter me, dig my place, help me with the difficult parts and love me. I quickly began to enjoy the job. I even thought that I was good, as good as they were, because they did not leave me behind. Digging became a joy to me and it seemed to me that they too enjoyed it. Rather than feeling the failure I thought I would be, I felt quite a success. I really believed that I had obtained a skill in digging and I developed a new attitude towards farm work.

As we worked the women also sang and talked. I cannot remember all the things that were said, but I do remember those that I had to report on to my mother. The group discussed and scheduled different ways to assist Berita. Some people volunteered to assist by fetching water for her from the river; others were to collect firewood, and a duty schedule was drawn up where at least one person would visit Berita every day. The group also talked about other people who needed various forms of assistance. They decided to go and sing and pray with one old woman who was bed-ridden. Her name was Mandela, the wife of Musa who was the church elder in our village. My mother used to spend endless hours at Mandela's bedside. Sometimes she took us children, and we watched as they talked and prayed. Mandela did not seem to be unhappy about her bed-ridden condition. She talked, she joked and she teased us. Sometimes she seemed very tired and just looked at us and smiled. It is no wonder to me that my younger sister is named after this woman who made such a big impact on my mother. Mandela's gift was prayer. When the women went to spend time with her, she was the one who challenged them to pray, to believe, to have hope in Jesus. She used to say that Jesus would soon come for her and that that was a good thing.

During the working time a number of women talked about various things that God was doing in their lives. We heard of healings from sickness; answers to prayers; blessings of all types. One woman thanked God that her maize was growing so well. Another for her children's performance at school. These things registered in my heart. I learnt that I needed to be thankful to God for the things in my life. As a teenager who was beginning to think that I was wiser than all these women put together, this one day changed my thinking. I have never forgotten it.

Today when I try to intellectualize my faith, my mind falters as I remember those women in my village, including Mandela, who were so thankful for every small thing in their life, and how they returned all the glory to God. I also remember how they passed on their faith to others in both words and deeds without creating special occasions and places for it. Today I remember something I took for granted then. While we worked on the farm, each one of the women shared something from the Bible. It was not by reading the scriptures. Someone would say that they had been going through some hardships and a certain scripture had helped them. They would re-tell the scripture to the others in a narrative way. There was always a great deal of attention being paid to what each person said. These women listened to one another. I did not know about bible study at that time. Now I realize that they were doing a bible study. There was no visible person leading the group. Still I sometimes try to wind the clock backwards looking for possibilities in my life today where sharing can be equal and mutual, where it does not need special leadership. How can we who lead learn to be unobtrusive and affirming to all others around us I keep asking myself.

Indeed, looking back at that encounter today and knowing that many of these women are still alive and helping one another and studying the scriptures unobtrusively I know that they are saints, evangelists, missionaries, teachers and counsellors although they will never be known by those names. I need to remember them and to name them on the tablet of my heart.

Evangelism

Having called the ushirika women's group evangelists and missionaries, there is a need to explore this further. In his acclaimed and voluminous work David B. Barret[2] argues vehemently that Africa has had the highest Christian growth in the last few decades. This shift of the centre of Christianity from the North to the South, has created many volumes of literature and hours have been spent at conferences attempting to explain it. For Africa in particular, suggestions for the spread of Christianity have ranged from mission work to the maturity of African Christianity as opposed to the aging of Western Christianity and there has even been the cynical remark that Africans are so notoriously and deeply religious that this phenomena should raise no eyebrows. Those who are cynical often see African religiosity as something springing out of primitive culture and therefore as a thing of the past. The ever-growing secularization of the West is then perceived as a sign of modernity and implicitly linked with development. The people in the developed world are very busy keeping their preciously-achieved development in tune through a work ethic that has no time for God, for others or even for self. Things must be done. Profit must be made. Time is money. Everybody is urged to succeed, succeed, and succeed.

Hence, the thing to do is to make sure that there is enough social security for everybody. Homes are built for the elderly; buildings are accessible for the physically handicapped; there are enough psychotherapists for the lonely; psychologists for those with questions and funeral homes equipped to attend to all the needs of the dead and the bereaved. Good works are being done and the list goes on. Once availability of comfort is achieved, everybody is on their own and God for no one (or is it God for all?).

The African village women's attraction to God and to the church cannot be simply explained as a reply to the lack of all these amenities and efficient systems. Neither can it be simply attributed to mission that has come of age. There is no need either to romanticize or idealize it as the 'in' thing which the North needs to learn and emulate from the South. The African village women's attraction to the Christian faith must first be seen in the light of God's grace and revelation through the scriptures and secondly as the willingness to believe in this God of the Bible, and to tell others about the newly-found joy. These women share the Good News of Jesus Christ not because they lack material prosperity but because it is news that is good and worthy of sharing. It is Good News, and it therefore needs to be shared with those with whom one lives day in and day out. It is Good News, and it is therefore not embarrassing to talk to a neighbour about it. Its goodness opens the doors for sharing. The Good News is so good that its sharing cannot be limited to specific places like the church or to special people like the clergy or evangelists trained in seminaries and bible schools.

The rural African women who combine their traditional cultural way of living with their acquired Christian heritage know that they must draw from their traditional religion in order to inform Christianity. Traditional African religion demands to be lived holistically. There are no specific spheres for religion. Religion is life. Christianity too is embraced on those terms, and therefore the reaching out to one another in need desires both the proclamation of the word and the sharing of gifts. They could be gifts of service to one another or gifts of the harvest or the gift of just being present for the other person.

Evangelistic work among African women may take place at the well when several women meet to draw water. They talk to one another. They pour out their day's problems, counsel one another and empty themselves ready to make room for the gospel to grow. It is very rare to hear the word 'loneliness' in the village situation. Yet, rather than our villages being seen as our universities in teaching us and informing our understanding of what it means to love a neighbour like oneself, our African village life is often dismissed as having nothing to offer either to the church or to civilization. Worse still, women's daily lives form no interest for study or notice. Our cities, based on cultures from across the seas become the point from which we see African success and even evangelism.

In an African village a common scene is finding women seated, laughing and braiding each others hair. In some hours, corn rows and exotic patterns decorate the heads of women of all ages, from children to the elderly. When I was at a mission school the braiding of hair was forbidden, not for the usual Pauline comments (I Timothy 2.9) but because the teachers said it was a waste of time. Some people still see it as a waste of time because it is a women's activity. Husbands shout at their wives for wasting time; gossiping and 'making hair'. But these hair-braiding ceremonies are also the meeting points of sharing, counselling, finding friendship and developing supportive networks among women. Often they are evangelistic opportunities. Even where the sharing of the text of the gospel is not the focus, women sitting together and oiling each other's head before and after the braiding is one of the deepest points of friendship. It is an anointing of sorts. It deepens the love between a mother and a daughter, between sisters, grandchildren and grandparents, and friends. It has the healing effect of touch. It has inherent possibilities within the Christian idea of the 'laying on of hands'. It is a good thing.

Even the now numerous commercial hair braiding kiosks in African cities are still oases of bonding friendships between women and they open possibilities for sharing life beyond the immediate hair-braiding task. Very often women establish their particular hairdresser to whom they go all the time. The hairdresser expects her usual clients. When they arrive, she is grateful not just for the money she gets, but for the sharing. Let me illustrate.

Amina was my hairdresser in Nairobi. For six years, Amina nurtured my braids, advising me on the latest and best care for braided hair. If I went to her stall and missed her, I always went back home and returned another day. We used to talk about our families or discuss current affairs. Amina also often shared with me a lot of what went on in her life and mind day in and day out as she braided women's hair. I listened and admired how articulate she was. Amina wanted to do something different, but her educational background did not present her with the opportunity for which she longed. Amina was not aware of the possibilities that existed in the city. One day I went to Amina with a newspaper that was advertising evening school for women and asked her if she could afford to go to school in the evening. Amina jumped at the opportunity and started doing evening secretarial and typing classes. True to her intelligence, Amina is now working in an office as a secretary and her dreams have been fulfilled. I miss her doing my hair, but I am so happy to see her confident in herself and having found something she enjoys doing. For me, this African freedom of sharing on a personal level has inherent evangelistic possibilities for sharing the news of Jesus Christ. When I am in a hair salon, I share in some ways and make it clear that Jesus Christ means Good News to me. I do not see my sharing the news about Jesus as being different to sharing news about my family. My earthly family is for me a mirror image of my membership in the family of God. When I see the shortcomings in my earthly family or culture, I look to the family of God for visions of goodness. I do not always find all the answers, but I find no discouragement either, because in the same way that I continue loving and talking about my family, so the call to be a child of God through Jesus Christ is a continuous process of searching, finding and celebrating (Luke 15).

The sharing of life and self among African village women has evangelistic potential because it is not hindered by rank, class or socio-economic status. It is a priesthood of all believers. For the ushirika women's group, working on a farm together creates no room for rank. Doing work which has no collar (white or blue) is the reality of most African village women. These women develop a form of ministry of their own.

This ministry is about sharing each other's lives and sharing Christ. It is sharing in the true sense; not simply giving and receiving. It is partnership in mission; mission here being to carry one another's burden. It is not a matter of some people sitting in meetings and making decisions for other people, but rather the whole group making commitments for themselves. The garden being dug becomes both the office space and the board room. It is also the church where the gospel is preached within the context of the priesthood of all believers. Here in this context of women's groups, the hearts and heads become the filing cabinets, the diaries, and the history books of things that have been done, need to be done and will be done.

The ushirika women's group is not unique to my village. Such women's groups are spread all over Africa. Their evangelistic strength is never mentioned, often it is taken for granted. Many of them exist under the umbrella of meeting to do work with their hands, such as digging, knitting or cooking, and thus their Christian witness in word is completely undervalued. But we surely need to start questioning the explanation of women being the majority in the pews of the churches simply because of the preaching they hear on Sundays from pastors who are mainly male. Is there a possibility that more women come to know Christ through the associations they have with one another? Many African women's groups organize their programmes in such a way that they give time to each other. Their life-style does not render itself to spending all their time rushing from one structural organization to another with words and papers. They are not too busy to evangelize among themselves because they simply do it in the context of their work where no boundaries exist. It is also notable that these groups share the message of God without inhibition. I have heard many of them say 'I want to tell you how Jesus was good to me'; Or 'I am so grateful to God for providing the money for school fees for my child!'; Or, 'I know that God understands my situation, my illness or my sadness'.

Loving someone or something gives freedom in all cultures to speak about that love without inhibitions. I have never heard people being inhibited about speaking about their loved ones, but the moment a person says they love Jesus Christ it becomes offensive and a sign of being insensitive, self-centred or fundamental. This inhibition however is not an issue for African village women in their own set-up. They share without borders. For them it is Christ without frontiers.

Other evangelists

Even though this contribution focuses on Christian evangelistic work, we need to underscore the fact that other faiths on the African continent have an equally high growth. Islam for example challenges Christianity quite closely. The lack of inhibitions in talking to one another is not a preserve of women nor is it a Christian trait. It is a practice common to the whole continent, men and women alike. The question 'how are you?' may be answered with the whole history of the individual's welfare, not as a sign of looking for sympathy but merely being human. Sharing must be truthful. Let me tell you another story.

I met Mzee Hussein on the plane from Nairobi to Accra. We sat together and naturally greeted one another not just with 'Hi' or 'Hello', but in the prolonged involved way as dictated by our culture. 'Mzee' in Swahili means 'elder'. I therefore use the title to show that Hussein was older than I. We travelled together for six hours and shared news about our families and our faiths. I had probably never before met such an enthusiastic evangelist as Hussein. He taught me so much about his Muslim faith that I developed respect for him and for Islam. I also gathered the courage to talk to him about my Christian faith. Both he and I understood that this sharing was not intended as an attempted conversion of one another. However, as we began to learn about each others' beliefs there was a potential of him converting me or vice versa. I respected him as someone who is sure of what he believes and thinks that it is worth sharing. My ecumenical engagement had almost trained me not to share my Christian faith in an enthusiastic manner, but Hussein's testimony of Islam challenged me and gave me the assurance that it was fine for me to speak about what Christ and the Christian faith meant to me. He discussed my faith with me and asked me questions just as I asked him. As we landed at our final destination, Hussein said these words to me: 'My daughter I am glad that you believe in God. Mohammed and Jesus Christ have led both you and me to paths to find God. We must not be distracted by the fact that you go to a church and I go to a mosque. God wants us to live in peace with one another. God bless you my daughter'. '*Mungu akubariki bintiwangu*'. This is a similar blessing to that which a father gives to a child in my culture. I valued it and felt blessed indeed.

When I look back on my time with Hussein, I know that if I had been looking and searching, I would probably have embraced his faith not because he forced me to, but because he was not inhibited from sharing with me about his God. I remember Hussein not just as an elderly Muslim man. I remember him as father, husband, grandfather, faithful believer, a retired government employee, an educated well-travelled intelligent person, a human being, and as an evangelist and a Muslim saint. He gave me a chance to learn about his journey of faith. I was challenged to do likewise. He blessed me.

Hussein represents to me another aspect of African holistic evangelism. The desire and the freedom to share self and faith go hand in hand. On the one hand our daily lives and experiences portray our need for the power and revelation of God. On the other hand, God's revelation and love for us has come to us through the love and grace which we embrace through faith and experience. As both of these merge into our total being they cannot be expressed separately. 'Our daily actions, behaviour, relationships and conversations must witness to both our lives and our faith. Sometimes this freedom of simply talking to one another becomes an evangelistic possibility and opportunity. In talking to one another, we become therapists, pastors and friends. Dom Helder Camara speaks about this more clearly.

> 'If we do not press the absurd claim of being the best, if we present ourselves as brothers and sisters for others, we shall be astounded to discover what a lot of people of goodwill there are about. Some of them may perhaps be rather timid, others will be so situated that they cannot see things in the same light as we do. But once they come across somebody who speaks from the heart, not seeking to impose anything on them or humiliate them, and not with the conviction of being any cleverer or holier, then they are affected and also join the march'.[3]

Christian evangelism must take the shape of ministry by realizing that the ministry of Christ is that of servanthood and self-sacrifice; the ministry of Christ is that of co-suffering with God's people; it is total obedience to the will of God; it is an urgent ministry requiring action here and now. The ministry of Christ is not of elevation, but of identification with the people to whom he came to minister, and it is about ministering to one another.

No one group of people can therefore be assigned this ministry or simply take it upon themselves. For we can never claim that certain people or occasions are better suited for service, for obedience or for action. Evangelism is service. Service is a gift of God. We are all called by the scriptures to offer our gifts in a variety of ways (Romans 12.3-8; I Cor. 12.4-11). Every Christian person is a co-worker in the proclamation of the gospel (Phil. 4.2-4). We will be judged not according to how we have hidden our talents for fear of the master, but rather, by how we have wisely utilized that which we have been given by God for the welfare of all creation. The ministry of evangelism is one that calls all of us to sainthood for Christ's sake. Those women in my village, the ushirika women's group, taught me evangelism. They are the saints in my life. Gardening, cooking, singing, studying, having babies, visiting the sick, and so many other daily events are the artifacts. These are the things which evoke memories of these saints in me. I must take them with me to church on All Saints Day.

Notes

1 *Newsweek*, November 12th 1990.
2 David B. Barret, *World Christian encyclopaedia: A comparative study of churches and religions in the modern world* (Oxford University Press, Nairobi/New York, 1982).
3 *Through the gospel with Dom Helder Camara* (Orbis Books, Maryknoll, 1986).

God's Good News in Europe Today

Reinhild Traitler

On the difficulty of discerning what God is doing

What God is doing is not a statement of fact, but a confession of faith. Even to ask the question already puts us into a context of faith. It implies that there is a willingness to discern in the events of our everyday lives 'that which is of God'. What God is doing is a matter of discernment, of the grace I am granted to discern. It is always linked to a context, to life itself. 'You cannot proclaim the love of God apart from an event' reads a poster of Brazilian cartoonist Claudio Ceccon. How and where I discern what God is doing today is linked to the events of my own life. I know why I see God on the side of the poor, the weak, those that cannot speak for themselves. It is connected to my own experiences of being in the minority, a Protestant in Catholic Austria. It has also something to do with those years in the ecumenical movement when the yearnings for justice of so many people became my own.

God is on the side of the poor

I still remember when I understood, with painful sharpness, that God is on the side of the poor. It was during my first visit to India, from the discreet comfort of a Swissair flight I had tumbled into the misery of an early morning slum in Bombay. It was another world, only I was the same, but I did not fit here, nor did my white middle-class God of German origin. All the impeccable sentences about this God were totally irrelevant to people for whom the love of God could only be translated into one decent meal per day, a cup of clean water and a minimum of human dignity. Then I realized that the gospel was only true to the extent that it could become concrete in our lives. It was not a matter of the right sentences about God, but discerning God there, in the midst of the people. It was the beginning of a search which continues to this day. Sharing the process of discernment of what God is doing in our lives is trying to find an answer to our own continuing question 'What is God doing?'. There may be hermeneutical surprises. We may find God at work where we had not looked. I have experienced this in my work with women in one of the richest countries of the world. We have to look carefully at the 'events', at the context, in which we live and move. God is not doing the same thing for everybody. The good news is not a universally applicable metaphysical truth, but one which is inextricably linked to the most profound needs and longings of people. Trying to discern 'what God is doing' in Europe today therefore means to understand what is happening in Europe at the beginning of the last decade of this century.

Looking at the events – where are we today in Europe?

Recently the Swiss woman clown Gardis Hutter received an award for her play 'Cheese'. 'Cheese' is a comic pantomime with a highly political message. It is about a poor little mouse who sits in her hole, hungry and peering in front of a large mousetrap which contains an enormously big cheese. There she sits watching the cheese with desire, greed and the intensity of hunger. Finally, she discovers that she can enter the mousetrap. It is so old and rusty that the mechanism does not function properly anymore. Soon we see the little mouse established inside the trap. The cheese has become much smaller and the mouse is now so fat that she can hardly move to put on her shoes. The trap too has changed. It is carpeted in yellow velvet and stuffed with the status symbols of affluence. The mouse has become a 'consumer', gobbling up everything, food, information, emotions. We watch the tremendous boredom of a life where every wish can be fulfilled, until one day the mouse discovers the full moon through her telescope and thinks it is a tremendous piece of cheese. She rushes through the audience, commanding some men to help her get the cheese down from the skies. While she is busy organising the audience the moon turns into a crescent. Our greedy mouse thinks the men have stolen her cheese. She starts accusing them, pleading with them, promising them payment. She rushes back to her trap, pulls down the remaining chunk of cheese to bribe the 'thieves', then the trap goes down. The play is a powerful metaphor for our own situation in Western Europe.

The trap goes down on our evergrowing greed to have more. It goes down on our lust for power and on our quest for material things. Could it be that we are sitting inside an enormous cage full of everything we could dream of, and yet it is impossible for us to walk beyond the wonderland of affluence, to extend our hands to our sisters and brothers outside, to share what we have and who we are?

Pictures for today

In the present situation in Europe it is difficult to think in such metaphors, because developments seem to point in another direction. The walls have come tumbling down and there is a feeling of freedom and openness. Europe is rapidly moving towards integration, and when we look at economic developments we could say that – at the level of the market – Western Europe is virtually integrated. It is the world that has made Western Europe 'ecumenical': People can buy the same products whether they shop in Göteborg or in Palma de Mallorca. They can expect the same services whether they drive along French highways or Austrian ones; they can watch the same TV programmes, cable networks, pay with the same credit cards and drink the same beer. With the creation of the single market these developments will be formalised, the cultural pulls will become stronger. Germans will retire in Spain and Spaniards will go to work in Germany, a single currency will be acceptable between Amsterdam and Athens and English will probably become the new Latin of the new Europe.

But this '*oikumene* of the market' does not extend into the former socialist countries as yet. The economies are not compatible. Apart from the standard and quality of goods in those countries, there were other priorities for production. The production of consumer goods was built around narrowly defined social needs, based upon such values as scarcity and austerity. Production in the affluent market economies of the West, however, is built around desires. Desires grow out of our need structure but they transcend it. They have something to do with our human longing for freedom, choice and abundance.

In terms of our economic situation in Europe we are non-contemporaries. The East is like the lean mouse that moves into the open trap, finally to get a share of that special cheese. The West is like the fat mouse that rushes towards the moon. At the moment, no discussion is possible about the cheese itself or about life in the trap. Those who have not yet had the privilege of consumption see in it an expression of freedom, as freedom is always the freedom you have not enjoyed yet. Those who have fed on it see the demise of real existing socialism as a vindication of the superiority of democratic market economies, and tend to overlook their structural shortcomings. While the challenges of socialism cannot be posed in classical Marxist language anymore, certain questions remain valid, such as the question of property, of the ownership of the means of production, and the assumption that human needs and human labour must be the basis for economic activity. The papal encyclical *Centesimus Annus* will make it even more difficult to pick up the debate on socialism, as it elevates the emerging global trend towards democratic market economies almost to the status of natural law; a form of economic, social and political organisation, inherent in human beings. Of course, the changes which have occurred in Europe over the past five years also give reason to rejoice. The Second World War has finally come to an end. The ideological struggle between socialism and capitalism which has taken so much energy and so many lives, is finally over. It looks as though a third way is emerging – social democratic market economies. Of course it is a third way for the rich. In most Third World societies crude and exploiting forms of capitalism continue as part of a structural arrangement that, in the final analysis, makes possible the economic redistribution in the different societies of Europe.

The past five years have accelerated a process that has been underway for decades, namely the integration of twelve European countries. The famous Norwegian peace researcher Yohan Galtung recently expressed the fear that the disappearance of a bipolar Europe could mean a future of uncontested hegemony of Western Europe. A Europe that stretches from Iceland to the Urals, with the Frankfurt Stock exchange established in Wolgograd, would indeed make us pause to redefine the winners and losers of the Second World War. Villagers in Spanish Galicia and those in the Outer Hebrides would alike crave for hamburgers and jeans and heavy metal rock.

Power and vulnerability

Yet, the very economic strength of the hegemonical power of Western Europe would also make for its vulnerability. Already there are frictions between the centres and the peripheries of the European Community (EC) countries themselves, between EC countries and those of the European Free Trade Association (EFTA), which is now being integrated into the European Economic area, and between both of these and the former socialist countries of Central and Eastern Europe. There are also various peripheries within the EC countries, such as the growing numbers of unemployed, migrant workers and 'new poor', especially older people and women. Indeed, certain economic trends seem to become sharper, as they are now being introduced into the former socialist countries. For instance, we see development around certain growth poles and uneven distribution resulting in social problems like unemployment misery and property crimes. At the same time, we can see an erosion of old cultural values, consumerism as a social attitude, and a certain nostalgia for the security that existed in socialist days, imperfect as that time was.

As this cannot be expressed in Marxist terms anymore, it may look for other ideological expressions, such as nationalism, religious fundamentalism, even fascism. Already we can see a tremendous increase of ethnic strife, old enmities and unresolved conflicts hidden by the pax sovietica come to the fore, often with violent force. The military element of the EC is presently being built around the need to have a European peace-keeping force that would quell such unrest and ensure a stable economic and political climate. As the unrest would presumably come from those whose aspirations have not been fulfilled as yet, such scenarios describe a process of 'Third Worldization' of large parts of Europe.

Of course other scenarios are possible. There could be a softer transition of the economically weaker countries of Europe into a Europe the shape of which would be defined in the framework of the Conference on Security and Co-operation in Europe (CSCE). There could be a culturally stronger axis between Central and Eastern Europe, maximum internal production in the East and strengthened trade ties between EFTA and the former socialist countries. Political decision making could be centred on CSCE, the North Atlantic Treaty Organisation (NATO) could be transformed into a largely political body, and the EC modelled as a federation of states rather than a union.

Unfortunately, within the last year events have precluded some of these possibilities. The decision concerning a central bank and a Common European currency point to the goal of the political union of the EC member states. The speed with which the EC has moved on these and other issues seems to preempt the process of CSCE. Furthermore, the urgency with which the EFTA countries have sought EC membership, and have already agreed on a common economic area, points in the same direction.

At the end of this century, which has been a century of European problems forced upon the world, we have to pause and ask ourselves 'What kind of future do we want for our continent?'. The kind of future I want is shaped by my closeness to those who are presently marginalized in Europe: migrant workers, refugees, asylum seekers; women who still work more for less pay, and who suffer discrimination in spite of constitutional amendments guaranteeing full equality; people in Eastern Europe who are threatened out of existence by the new situation and communities in the Third World who may be the ultimate losers in the new hegemonical arrangements now being developed.

Is there a challenge for us as European Christians to be involved in the process of integration, and, if so, in what way? As Europeans and as Christians we carry the burden of a history of conquest and of exploitation. For too long European Christians have spoken of the love of God and have carried the sword. As Europe wishes to be a superpower again there is only one place where Christians can legitimately be: at the side of those trampled underfoot by the process; working actively for a European order in which the best of our traditions, human rights, social democracy, enlightenment and freedom for all, can become a reality; resisting any gigantomania and self-righteousness that smack of a 21st century repetition of the colonial blunders of five hundred years ago.

Proclaiming the good news means doing God's will

I have tried to sketch 'the events', the context in which I live and work in Europe, within which I have to make choices, where I try to be faithful. If the love of God should not remain metaphysics, a spiritual 'added value' which can be attached to any situation, if it is to be transforming power, then sharing God's life-giving word means actually doing it. I can only discern what God is doing as I get involved in God's work. Alone I cannot do it. I have to join others. In our common commitment I have met 'God', I have seen that which is of God in other people, their deepest longings for justice, their capacity to love, their dedication to live in peace. In our common spiritual journey in the peace movement and in the women's movement we have rediscovered some of the values of our Christian tradition which could help in the process of European integration, and which could be guidelines for our personal lives. Doing God's will is a life discipline, for which we need to develop additional spiritual resources.

I would like to share some of these values:

The value of smallness

Smallness is a value not so much in an aesthetic sense ('small is beautiful'), but in an existential sense. When we are small, we are close to the earth, we see what is 'down there', the suffering and the powerlessness of little people. Smallness is a gospel value. Jesus is close to the little people and their seemingly little problems; poverty, hunger, illness, discrimination, lack of love. This is the stuff of which life is made, and which is easily forgotten in the parlours of the great and mighty.

I wish that the churches in Europe would have the courage to become small; or that they would have the guts to admit that they are small in terms of their influence; that they would use smallness as a chance to be absolutely honest and exercise the prophetic ministry of which they have so often been afraid for fear of losing money and power. Europe needs to be reminded that the most noble task of the big and strong is to listen to and safeguard the rights of the small and to create conditions that will help them to live side by side with the strong.

The justice values of the Torah

From my Jewish friends I have learned that justice is paramount, and that it must be concrete. It is not a matter of vague feelings, but one of rights. In the Torah justice means a system of clearly defined rights, particularly for those that suffer: the poor, the slaves, the widows and orphans, the aliens. Justice means that they too have a right to food and shelter, to protection, to life in the community. This is clearly shown in the laws governing the treatment of widows, orphans and strangers, or the concept of the sabbath and Jubilee years which aim at the restitution of freedom, the cancellation of debts and rest for the earth.

What is important is that the Torah formulates a system of obligations and rights. It is not a question of charity, but one of rights. Can our churches think and act on the basis of human rights rather than on the lines of charity, of voluntary giving and diakonical work? Are we ready to extend to Palestinians, Turks and Greeks in our midst the same human rights that we enjoy in our respective nations (the Torah does!).

The values of the Sermon on the Mount

Some years ago a German political journalist discovered the Sermon on the Mount and wrote a book, *Love is possible.* It claims that the Sermon on the Mount is not only for dreamers but can be enacted in everyday life. Of course, when we look at the blessings of Jesus and at 2,000 years of Christian practice, we may lose heart. Can we put the Sermon on the Mount at the centre of our spiritual basis for a new Europe? Can we 'rescue' the blessings from misinterpretations?

'Blessed are the peacemakers' Jesus said (Matt. 5.9) and too often this has been seen as saying that blessed are those that have peace at heart, or peace in the private sphere, where the public dimension of the peacemaking task has been underestimated and even forgotten. Our tradition has excelled in developing theological publications for war, but it has not brought forth, until very recently, concepts of peace with justice.

Can we provide a political interpretation to the blessing announced for those pure in heart? The pure in heart are those that can discern in the other person the image of God. Only those who are pure in heart will be able to see the good in other people. This is a much needed corrective to the popular capitalist anthropology, which suspects love in human beings and which echoes the Roman *homo homini lupus* (human beings are wolves to each other). It also reflects a simplistic understanding of the theological concept of the sinfulness of all creatures. Those 'pure in heart' have doubts about this concept: they can see something of the goodness of Creation before the Fall still present in the created order. They believe there is something incorruptible present in every living being, and that that something is of God. The pure in heart could show us how to love our enemies, how to respect creation and how to care for this earth, our only home.

The values of scarcity and of voluntary simplicity

Scarcity has always been a value in the Christian tradition. The Jesus movement itself was most probably one of shared scarcity. Later the monastic orders took on the ideal of voluntary poverty. Riches were seen as a hindrance on the way to the kingdom. You cannot serve God and mammon. In a secularized form scarcity became a virtue in early capitalism. It was the means by which money for investments was amassed. In the developed economies of Europe however, scarcity should not be introduced as a means of saving for new investments. Rather it ought to be linked to the care of creation, to the protection of Europe's exhausted environment and to sharing justly with the countries of the two-thirds World. Also, these values do not apply in the same way to everybody in Europe. Scarcity and simplicity are values that need to be practised first of all by affluent Europe.

Solidarity and sharing

We have reason to fear that Europe could become a megapower on the backs of the people of the poor world. At the World Council of Churches (WCC) convocation on Justice, peace and the integrity of creation, Christians from the Third World shared with us their concern that European churches were so pre-occupied with the new needs in Eastern Europe and with the process of European integration that they had become oblivious to the worsening situation in other parts of the globe. I believe that in spite of the many challenges in Europe we have to keep global solidarity before our eyes.

A Europe of many cultures and religions

What does this mean in view of the fact that the United States of America and Europe (in the framework of the United Nations and with the help of some African and Asian nations) have just fought and won a war against an Islamic state, which was also a war over the control of vital economic resources. What does it mean in the face of militant Islam, the attraction of Asian religions and the fascination with obscure sects. I firmly believe that Europe can no longer be a 'fortress of Christianity'. A 're-Christianization' of Europe is full of echoes of the suffering of the countless people who became victims of the unholy alliance between the love of Christ and the love of power. It can only serve the cause of Christ by acknowledging that there are other revelations of God and by practising the human right to religious and cultural freedom. At the same time Christians must be prepared to speak a clear word of witness. Life together will be enhanced in that way. It does not help to gloss over differences or to pretend that we are all the same. We are not all the same. As Christians we proclaim God in very different ways. Our concepts of human life, of freedom, and of community differ radically. It is necessary to learn and to know this, so that mutual understanding can grow.

I have sketched some guidelines for our spiritual discipline of 'doing God's will'. But how do we do it? My own personal longing is for a transformation of our churches, because they are, in spite of all short-comings (which are actually our own), still a global network, a community of people that share a very simple faith: God loves each one of us, God wanted each one of us, God made me in God's image, God again and again accepts me in all my weakness. But: God is Father and Mother of all, of the neighbour I love and of the enemy I despise. This faith provides for us a bond and responsibility. The bond is between all. All are sisters and brothers, rich and poor alike. The responsibility therefore is to shake the powerful on their thrones, to empower the powerless, and to help those in between to take sides – with love. We can do this, because Jesus Christ did it before us, and because he understands the suffering this may involve. We can do this, because we are not alone – we are with each other, and God's spirit is among us. We also share the new life in humility and courage.

Doing God's will

In humility and courage the churches in Europe could be present in shaping anew the continent. Doing God's will at the present moment may involve two commitments:

A commitment to 'reconciliation' with the past

1992 will not only mark the establishment of the single market but also 500 years of conquest. Is there any other way of celebrating this than a public confession of sin? Can we turn around, before there is a point of no return. The Swiss churches proclaimed 1991, the 700th anniversary of the Swiss confederation, a Jubilee year, where debts should be released, where Swiss Christians commited themselves to save energy and where the churches would strive to establish an alternative to military service. On the basis of a petition from the churches, the first of these goals has been reached: Swiss parliament cancelled 700 million Swiss Francs worth of debts on national bank credits. These are concrete steps towards reconciliation. Can the churches in the former colonial powers of Europe do the same?

A commitment to qualify the process of European integration

It is the churches who could insist on a vision that takes up the best of the traditions of East and West – justice and freedom. This vision could find its secular expression in the adoption of a truly comprehensive set of human rights for all of Europe, in the framework of a truly democratic process.

The churches could make a conscious option for the poor and the powerless in this continent, and divert energies and resources towards giving them space, including them in their decision-making bodies and encouraging the development of European theologies of liberation. This will not scare away the wealthy; on the contrary, it might well turn into a healing experience for all, because our souls cannot be healed by an 'added value spirituality'. We will be healed only to the extent that we discover the needs and yearnings in the face of our brothers and sisters.

If we do this we will grow to be truly open communities. I experience these in the women's church, the communities of women and men that try to live and worship and strive for the kingdom as a community of equals. There is nothing to be feared. We have been richly endowed. The future is not to be fat mice in a cage, but to move out, to bow down and to discover God's image in others – in all.

The Words of the Excluded A Study on Mark 7.24-30

Raquel Rodriguez

Nearly two centuries of interpretations by others have inevitably influenced the manner in which Christians in Latin America read the accounts of Jesus' ministry. Although the interpretations are valid, we have noticed that these readings have taken away part of the flavour and impact from the message intended through the actions and didactic methods used by Jesus in each case.

We would like to read this passage using the most important hermeneutical key for reading and re-reading every passage of the Bible: the central message of the gospel of Jesus Christ, 'I have come that they may have life, and have it to the full' (John 10.10). Along with it we do not want to pass by the particular elements highlighted by this passage.

Working with additional hermeneutical keys

Scandal

We believe 'scandal' as a key allows for the discovery of important elements in this particular passage. We have become accustomed to listening to accounts of the gospel to the point that we know them by heart. This has made us miss their scandalous dimension. The rediscovering of the scandalizing elements of the passage can give us a better understanding of Jesus' ministry that ended in the scandal of the cross.

All four gospels present Jesus' ministry by narrating and emphasizing the parts considered most important, so that the central message of the ministry, death and resurrection of Jesus Christ might have an impact on God's people. They all kept the scandalous elements and, even though some softened the situations in their descriptions [see for example, the difference between Matthew and Mark on the passage we are studying (Mark 7.24-30, Matt. 15.21-28)], the element of scandal was not erased from the texts because it is an integral part of Jesus' ministry (cf. Mark 3.1-6 also).

What has happened is that we are not used to reading the passage based on this key, and our reading, therefore, softens the scandal. Scandal is very important for understanding certain elements of the mandate entrusted to us by Jesus Christ for the mission of the church and for each one of us. By discovering scandals, we can also understand how the church has permitted certain situations, both within itself and in its mission, that can distract from the central message of the gospel, for example, the scandal of Jesus' acceptance and promotion of women as his disciples and their active participation in the primitive church. They later became marginalized from this position because the church allowed the values and ethics of the surrounding society to act as guidelines instead of the scandalous elements of Jesus' ministry.

Miracles

In our very rational and scientific society, the miracles of exorcism and physical healing are not treated with due respect. We try to find a rational, logical and scientific explanation for them, thereby weakening the message of the event itself.

Miracles, as part of Jesus' ministry, are related to the central message of the reign of God: **life and life in abundance.** Exorcism and the healing of sickness are inter-related. Both illness and demon-possession were believed to be caused by sin either committed by the person themselves, their parents, or their ancestor (cf. John 9.1ff, about the healing of the man that was born blind; Luke 13.10ff, the healing of the bent over woman). Sickness was considered a sign of demon possession and, therefore, the person who was either sick or possessed was deprived by society from the possibility of an abundant life. This happened particularly in the city of Jerusalem where men with any sort of disease could not practise religious rituals inside the Temple. Sick people were separated from daily social activities. Depending on the type of illness (for example, leprosy and diseases related to blood-flow in women), the person was not only rejected, but completely isolated as well.

Being sick was equivalent to being demon-possessed. In many cases of exorcism recorded by the gospels, it was actually a physical illness perceived as a demon possession as in the case of the bent over woman mentioned above.

When Jesus heals or exorcizes, he not only takes away the pain and discomfort these persons have, he also makes possible their reincorporation in society and religious practice, giving them the opportunity to live an abundant life. Therefore, the message behind miracles goes far beyond a magical kind of exorcism or healing; they become signs and first fruits of the message of the reign of God: the possibility of a full and abundant life.

Based on these three inter-related hermeneutical keys: the message of the announcement of full and abundant life; scandals; and miracles, we would like now to re-read the passage of the encounter of the Syrophoenician woman with Jesus in Mark 7.24-30.

The Drama

Stage where the action takes place

The place where this event occurs is relevant to the understanding of the scandal behind the plot. After walking and preaching in Galilee, near the border, Jesus leaves Galilee and enters the non-Jewish territory of Tyre.

Characters

This passage has three characters. As Jesus arrives in Tyre, a woman appears to him who is described as being from that same place, therefore Syrophoenician and also a non-Jew (the text refers to her as a pagan). Although never actually on the scene, the woman's daughter is an integral part of this drama. She is probably not older than twelve years as verse 30 refers to her as a child and, according to Jewish society, a child became a woman at twelve years of age.

Plot

Jesus had been involved in heated discussions with the Pharisees in Galilee and had therefore crossed the border in order to rest. He arrived at a house hoping to be unnoticed. There he finds the woman, Syrophoenician and pagan. She recognizes him and begs him to cast out an evil spirit from her daughter. Jesus refuses abruptly, but she implores vehemently. Jesus then, responds to her plea by sending her home with the assurance that her daughter is cured. Upon arrival, she finds the girl well and resting in her bed.

A reading based on the three proposed hermeneutical keys

If we only read as far as the plot is concerned, we would find ourselves with nothing more than another of Jesus' miracles and we would miss some of the fundamental teachings of this lesson.

In the first place, let us take a look at the miracle itself. It is a miracle of exorcism. According to the mother, the girl has been possessed by a demon. It could probably refer to either a physical illness or a mental illness, we do not have that information. What we do know is that, from the hermeneutical key concerning miracles, this girl does not have the possibility of life in abundance and is therefore suffering. Her condition does not allow her to participate fully in daily social life, and she must be liberated so that she would be able to fully live. For this reason, the mother implores Jesus, recognizing in him the possibility of a miracle that can give the girl a chance to live a worthy life. The miracle takes place. So far, so good.

Things become a little more complicated, however, when we read this passage from the hermeneutical key concerning scandal. In this respect, we cannot help being scandalized when, in spite of the woman's pleading, Jesus refuses to accede to her.

A traditional reading of this passage moves quickly from the mother's plea to Jesus' announcement that an exorcism has taken place in the body of the girl and then immediately to the proof that the miracle has been fulfilled. The reason for this is that, if we should stop and pay attention to the dialogue, we would be scandalized because in it we would not be able to find the traditional image we have of Jesus Christ.

In this case, the scandal is not on the part of Jesus towards the Pharisees and Sadducees of his time, but towards us. It scandalizes us to think of Jesus refusing to give this girl the opportunity of life in abundance, because we know that he could do it with no trouble whatever. It scandalizes us to see him giving priority to the interests of the Jews (the chosen people), and not to the plea of this mother on behalf of her child's life. It scandalizes us to hear Jesus referring to a person as a 'dog', or 'little dog', as Mark tries to soften it, especially when referring to a woman and a mother who is humiliating herself to the point of risking rejection, only because, to her, her daughter's life is much more important than what Jesus and other people around her might think or say about her.

The scandal of Jesus comparing this woman with a 'dog' has always been concealed in traditional readings by stating that the Jews refer to all pagans as dogs, in accordance with the tradition of their times (cf. Paul in some of his letters, uses this term to refer to pagans also). We can, of course, accept this explanation, but that does not lessen the impact of the rudeness of comparing a person with a dog and, in this case, the denigrating implications for a woman who is humiliating herself and begging Jesus to give her daughter the possibility of living an abundant life.

This is not the end of the scandal. The woman, a mother in constant struggle, actually dares to refute Jesus' words. This was a scandal for the society where it actually happened, and it is a scandal for us too. In those days, it was unheard of for a woman to contradict a man, still more a stranger, and especially in public: and refuting an argument was worse than anything else. For us, that Jesus was this man is also scandalous. But what is even more scandalous is what happens after the Syrophoenician woman refutes Jesus' argument.

When Jesus refuses the Syrophoenician girl the chance of a worthy life, he does it based on the argument that she does not belong to the chosen people. Not only is she not a Jew by birthright, but neither is she Jewish by embracing the Jewish faith. The woman's argument is that, without taking away what belongs to the chosen, others may have access to the life that is proclaimed by the announcement of the reign of God, because the reign of God is not to be enjoyed by the chosen alone. The woman, accustomed to being considered inferior, asks for just a little part, the 'crumbs'. She is not interested in selfishly displacing others; she only asks for a little and not even for herself.

The major scandal takes place at this moment. The woman, by means of her word and therefore her argument, converts Jesus. She evangelizes him. She makes him understand that the reign of God and the Good News that he proclaims go a lot further than what he had imagined until then. And a new scandal takes place again. The miracle is not carried out by Jesus. The miracle is performed by the woman. 'Because of this saying you may go your way; the demon has gone out of your daughter' (verse 29). This is the only miracle in the gospels that does not come directly from Jesus, as it obeys, instead, the argument of the Syrophoenician woman. It is the word of the foreign woman, the pagan, the excluded: the voice of the voiceless, that does the miracle.

Is this scandal not something worth recovering? Not for putting down the image of Jesus Christ, but to rediscover his sensitivity and ability to adjust his preaching and ministry to the greatness of the reign of God. Jesus opens his own eyes to a greater reality. He who had fought against religious practices that were not part of the central message of the gospel by the announcement of a full and abundant life, is confronted by a woman who warns him not to limit the magnitude of God's reign. Jesus allows himself to be evangelized by this woman, whom he had called a 'dog' and to whom he had denied the first fruits of the reign of God. She is the main character of this story, and Jesus recognizes it and gives her credit. She is the one that performs the miracle giving back the possibility of life in abundance to her daughter and evangelizing Jesus.

Reading the passage from the point of view of the excluded in Latin America

The reading of this passage from our own hermeneutical keys, and a re-reading based on Latin American experience allows us to open new horizons and to feel the message of the reign of God closer to us.

Drastic changes have been taking place in the world during the past years (the end of the eighties and the beginning of the nineties) such as the end of the cold war, the destruction of the Berlin Wall, the unification of Europe and its new configuration as of 1992 around the European Community, and the crisis of the historical Socialism. But in spite of all these changes, Latin America continues to be a region of excluded people.

The depredation of our environment and the systematic pauperization to which our communities have been subjected, have no end. This has been our reality for almost five hundred years, and now we are asked to celebrate with joy these five hundred years of exclusion!

As Europe celebrates its economic unification, our reflection from within Latin America will not be around the encounter of two cultures, but rather on the enslavement of our cultures, our communities, our people, our land, our natural resources, by a foreign culture. We will be commemorating five hundred years of resistance of our indigenous people against cultural and economic depredation. We will be commemorating resistance against exclusion from the possibility of worthy life, and we will be celebrating our ability to survive.

When the Europeans came to our lands, they believed they had arrived at other lands. They were lost but were not aware of it until years later. Nevertheless, when they discovered the possibilities of economic and international power represented by the domination of these lands, they did not hesitate at all in taking possession not only of our land, but also of our richness and our people. Realizing that they could not reach their ambitious goals using the people of our lands, they brought black brothers and sisters from Africa, to do the work our people would not, or could not, do.

Not pleased with all this, and in the name of God and Jesus Christ, they 'evangelized' us forcefully, without taking into account our religious beliefs and sensitivities. They forced us to become Christians under the threat of death. Nonetheless, because of our colour, and our surviving culture our framework continued to be different. We have never stopped being the excluded, the 'dogs' of the passage we are studying.

Reading the passage from the framework of our experience, we find that Jesus left his land to go to a foreign land (Tyre), where he met a pagan woman: the excluded from the chosen people, the 'dog'. The Europeans came to our lands and in the name of what they believed was the true gospel, continued to consider us as being excluded, as the 'dogs'. As with the Syrophoenician woman at the beginning of the passage we have been excluded not only by the European colonization but also, in the present times, by the international economic and political order.

How can we read this passage in order for it to bring Good News to the excluded people of Latin America? Reading it from our own context, it can offer us the strength we need to continue struggling for survival and empower us to struggle for the opportunity of abundant life announced by the reign of God.

The Syrophoenician woman personifies our people, suffering and anguished by our own situation of the negation of life. Our demons and illness are hunger, disease (Western illnesses such as measles are killing our indigenous people and the cholera epidemic is called the sickness of the poor), unemployment; lack of housing, lands to cultivate, access to education and health programmes; depredation of our resources and natural wealth; the foreign debt, structural adjustment programmes, the market economy and neo-liberal policies. This woman, like our women, has a daughter that is suffering and she would do anything she could to restore her to a worthy life, as our women do anything they can to make it possible for their children to survive surrounded by death. All the Syrophoenician woman asks, and all we ask is that which has already been offered to us in the message of the Good News.

Our people, excluded from the worldwide political and economic order, ask for nothing else than the possibility of having access to life in abundance: but the international order responds that we are excluded and, without even softening the term as Mark did, constantly reminds us that we are 'dogs'.

Just as the woman in the story, we would like to refute the international political and economic system. We do not seek to take away what belongs to others (in spite of the fact that those others snatched away what belonged to us), but rather to live in great respect and justice, which would enable us to have access to worthy life.

The text gives us strength to refute the authorities and empowers us to feel that if Jesus could be evangelized by this woman excluded from his ministry, we can at least give it a try.

We do not intend to compare Jesus with the powers behind the system. Jesus came to proclaim life and is therefore sensitive to anything working against it. The passage shows that it was not very difficult for the Syrophoenician woman to convince him. In contrast, we know it is not an easy task to convince the powers behind the international political and economic system, because life in abundance for all is of no interest to them. The god they serve is not the God who sent Jesus Christ to announce the Good News of abundant life. Their god is an idol – the god of money and power – Mammon. For this god, the life of the majority is of no value at all. However, the evangelization carried out by the excluded woman in the passage gives us the hope and strength to attempt it. We do not want the crumbs under the table, though. We want to eat from the plate that is on top of the table, as it was granted to the daughter of the Syrophoenician woman. We must knock down the idols of the system and implant the God of Life. This will be our evangelizing task in Latin America. What will be yours?

Sharing the Good News of what God is doing Today

Kosuke Koyama

The Lord is merciful and gracious

> The Lord is merciful and gracious, slow to anger and abounding in steadfast love (Psalm 103.8, Exodus 34.6).

Because the Lord is merciful and gracious, we may be able to see what God is doing today. The church confesses that God is reconciling the world to Godself (2 Cor. 5.19). What is this reconciliation to God? At the heart of God's reconciliation stands Jesus Christ, 'the Lamb of God, who takes away the sin of the world' (John 1.29). Because God is steadfast love, God is, in Christ, taking away the sin of the world.

God who loves the world so much is concretely involved in what is happening in our world (Amos 9.7). As Jeremiah counsels we participate in what God is doing.

> For if you truly amend your ways and your doings, if you truly execute justice one with another, if you do not oppress the alien, the fatherless or the widow, or shed innocent blood in this place, and if you do not go after other gods to your own hurt, then I will let you dwell in this place, in the land that I gave of old to your fathers for ever (7.5-7).

In his parable of the Good Samaritan (Luke 10.29-37) Jesus commands us to 'Go and do likewise'. In the mind of Jesus when we 'go and do' the things that Jeremiah is speaking about, for instance, we are participating in the healing work of reconciliation in which God is engaged. We are in the Christ's mysterious way making concrete the mighty divine word in the world. 'Rise, take up your pallet and walk'.

> Which is easier, to say to the paralytic, 'Your sins are forgiven,' or to say 'Rise, take up your pallet and walk'? But that you may know that the Son of Man has authority on earth to forgive sins (Mark 2.9-10).

This is the mystery of the authority of Jesus Christ according to the apostolic faith. Christ has freedom to say either 'Your sins are forgiven' or 'Take up your pallet and walk'. With him these two calls are interchangeable, and the divine work in today's world is at once forgiveness and justice.

In this freedom of Christ Christians find the foundation for social responsibility. In Christ, the God who is working 'vindication and justice for all who are oppressed' (Psalm 103.6), is the God who is forgiving humanity's sins. To this Christians respond sincerely with the words, 'Lord, have mercy' (Luke 18.13). Christian theology and Christian ethics are united in our cry, 'Lord, have mercy'. Then, when we say 'Lord, have mercy' we are sharing the good news of what God is doing in the world today.

Concretely speaking . . .

I participate in a midnight run to visit homeless people in Lower Manhattan. We carry in our vans four hundred sandwiches, chicken soup, hot chocolate, lemonade, tooth brush/paste, blankets, underwear, trousers, shoes, socks and soap. All these things are prepared every week by two churches in New Jersey. Our first stop is under the Brooklyn Bridge. Here, beneath the flow of heavy traffic, homeless people live. Oblivious of their presence drivers overhead view a large billboard 'Dream house! a big bargain from $200,000. Don't miss it!' Luxurious condominiums are being built one after another, while the number of homeless people in the city is steadily increasing. Homelessness is, however, not just for those under Brooklyn Bridge. Homelessness comes to all of us when we ignore Jeremiah's counsel.

We are systematically destroying our most basic home, the planet earth. Etymologically, 'ecology' means 'home-understanding'. We have produced an ecological crisis, a 'home-crisis'. Destroying our planetary home, we are becoming homeless. 'If you do justice to the earth, I will let you dwell on the earth.'

Racism makes thirty million black people in the United States spiritually homeless by threatening their human dignity even though they may have a physical home with sandwiches and chicken soup. In the same way, sexism defiles the domicile of one half of the population of humanity. 'If you do not shed innocent blood, I will let you dwell on the earth.'

The twentieth century has seen unprecedented uprooting of peoples and homelessness. All over the world and particularly in Africa we see large scale refugee movements due to famine, war and oppressive regimes. Two world wars and countless local wars have made this century the most murderous and uprooting. In the midst of all this homelessness, we listen eagerly for the encouraging word of the Holy Spirit, 'Take up your pallet and walk'.

Homelessness

What are some of the causes of homelessness?

- Economic injustice on a global scale: A great majority of human beings are brutally exploited by the dominant group. Humanity today suffers from a cruel maldistribution of wealth.

- Parochial spirituality: Our parochial loyalties must be constantly challenged by the greater universal value. Patriotism is too often a narrow national parochialism that provides a whitewash for a nation's self-idolatry.

- Racism and sexism: As the ranks of the homeless swell in the United States we are seeing disproportionate numbers of single female parents and blacks entering them.

- Wars: The amount of human and natural resources that have been wasted in the preparation and execution of wars in our century staggers the imagination. Wars destroy homes.

- The destruction of the biosphere: The fundamental welfare of human life is being threatened by the destruction of the life-support system of the planet itself. Not only are our domestic homes being destroyed but our cosmic home is also being destroyed.

Against these demonic powers that produce homelessness, we read a passage from Deuteronomy:

> . . . when the sun goes down, you shall restore to him the pledge that he may sleep in his cloak and bless you; and it shall be righteousness to you before the Lord your God (24.13).

What 'a light murmuring sound' that is! (1 Kings 19.22). Yet, it penetrates the heart of human morality. These picturesque words express God's concern for the minorities, the weaker members of the community. Everyone is entitled to have the safety and comfort of a home at night. This must be the foundation for our political and economic activities. The welfare of people on the periphery is the central concern of God. When we 'restore to him the pledge . . .', only then will we experience the power of the redemption of God: 'Behold, the Lamb of God, who takes away the sin of the world'. How concrete the biblical faith is!

The homeless God

Our focus is to share the Good News of what God is doing today. God is working against the powers that make people homeless. Here, however, we are encountered by the strange 'homeless' God of the Bible. God became homeless because of God's love towards humanity.

> Thus says the Lord: Would you build me a house to dwell in? I have not dwelt in a house since the day I brought up the people of Israel from Egypt to this day, but I have been moving about in a tent for my dwelling (2 Sam. 7.5-6).

These words must not be understood as an insignificant comment about the nature of God. They express the fundamental character of the biblical God. The biblical God is a mobile, not a stationary, God. 'I am who I am' (Exod. 3.14) means 'I will be with you wherever you go'. When people walk three miles an hour, God walks three miles an hour. This is the meaning of the name of God (Exod. 3.13). Embodying the mind of this merciful and gracious God, Jesus Christ 'tented among us'.

> And the Word became flesh and dwelt (tented) among us (John 1.14).

> Foxes have holes, and birds of the air have nests; but the Son of man has nowhere to lay his head (Luke 9.58).

In this tented Jesus we find the foundation of the biblical concept of 'home'. Jesus Christ stands for 'God with us' (Matt. 1.23). 'The Word (Jesus Christ) was with God' (John 1.1). This provides the image of the most sacred divine home. 'God with us' creates homes, both personal and cosmic. Sociologically speaking, if we cannot pay the rent we become homeless. Theologically speaking, when we reject the 'God who is with us', we become homeless.

There is an astounding moment in the New Testament when Jesus who embodies 'God with us' becomes most profoundly homeless as he cries out on the cross, 'My God, my God why hast thou forsaken me?' (Mark 15.34).

No one has ever been made more homeless than Jesus. No one has ever been more on the periphery than Jesus. In the perception of the apostolic faith this forsakenness (homelessness) that Jesus experienced is the ultimate one. And this is the ultimate way in which God in Christ indicated God's concern for the whole creation. It is the most peripherized one who could embrace the whole creation. 'Behold, the Lamb of God who takes away the sin of the world'.

Paul affirms his apostleship as he speaks of his own life on the periphery:

> To the present hour we hunger and thirst, we are ill-clad and buffeted and homeless (unsettled) . . . (1 Cor. 4.11).

The qualification for his apostleship is hidden in his imitation of Christ's homelessness. This imitation of Christ includes the apostolic life style that he describes:

> When reviled, we bless; when persecuted, we endure; when slandered, we try to conciliate; we have become, and are now, as the refuse of the world, the offscouring of all things (1 Cor. 4.12-13).

When reviled, we bless – this is eucharistic and points to the impassioned words of Jesus: 'This is the body which is given to you'. It is the same spirituality that inspired a powerful non-violent civil rights movement led by Martin Luther King Jr. His movement followed the spirit of the Holy Communion. 'When reviled, we bless' – then we are genuinely 'homed'. Through the life of a people characterized by the apostolic life of 'when reviled, we bless' God is making all things new (Rev. 21.5).

The biblical faith is not romantic. We are called upon to be discerning. One late night under the Brooklyn Bridge an ambulance came just in time for a homeless woman to be taken to a hospital to deliver a baby. There is no apostolic quality in living under a bridge in dangerously unsanitary conditions. The African theologian Manas Buthelezi says that 'not all suffering is redemptive. Most of the suffering in the world is oppressive'. Homeless persons in a capitalist society experience outright human indignity. Jesus Christ stands against the human power that makes people physically uprooted and homeless.

Christian words must be concrete. It takes four hundred sandwiches to ease the hunger of four hundred homeless people. God is doing something through these sandwiches that the American B2 bomber, with a pricetag of eight hundred and fifty million dollars, cannot do. (The bomber is appropriately called a 'stealth' bomber, which literally means 'thievery'.) Who can eat the bomber and satisfy his or her hunger? A ten dollar blanket can keep a person under Brooklyn Bridge warm. That is more than any atomic submarine can do.

The Ecumenical God

The homeless God is the ecumenical God, the God of the whole world. This connection was established when Jesus Christ tented among us. This connection is Good News for us all. What does the connection mean?

Centrality of Periphery

What is the church? This question must be answered in the light of the

Christ who has been most peripherized. In the apostolic proclamation the Christ who was utterly forsaken and crucified is the head of the church and the world (Col. 1.15-20). The image of 'periphery' has a strong theological meaning because Jesus Christ was there – at the periphery.

One of the key phrases of the ecumenical movement is the 'people of God'. Who are the people of God when we say: 'For the people of God' in the liturgy of holy communion? There is a blessed ambiguity here. Are only baptized Christians the people of God? How about all the other people, whoever they are? Are they not people of God also? The bridge between the church and the world is hidden in Christ who has been to the extreme periphery. This is Christ's good news for all humanity.

God in Christ is creating a new horizon for the church today. Everyday we are challenged to experience that the reign of God is a far greater reality than we have been accustomed to think of in terms of our own image of the church. The church is built upon the 'homeless' Christ (John 1.11) and because Christ is homeless, Christ is universal.

This universality is not grasping (Phil. 2.6). It is free and therefore it emancipates us from egocentric exclusiveness, 'God, I thank thee that I am not like other men . . .' (Luke 18.11). The corporate Prayer of Confession said in Riverside Church in New York City (5 August 1990) expresses our Christian understanding of a universal God.

> O thou who hast made us for joy and not for sorrow, forgive us that the cities which we build are so heavily marked by fear and death. Behind bolted doors we sit, neither seeking our neighbour's good nor finding our own. We look but do not see. We hear but do not listen. We crowd but do not touch. We read but do not feel. Forgive us our sins, O Lord. Lengthen our reach. Broaden our sympathies. And help us, as Jesus loved Jerusalem, to love this city that we call our home. In his strong name we pray.

When we are encountered by the homeless/ecumenical God the words from our mouths are 'Forgive us our sins, O Lord. Lengthen our reach. Broaden our sympathies'. When we say this we are sharing the Good News of God in Christ who reached us and sympathized with us (John 3.16).

Critique of idols

The homeless/ecumenical God is a radically open God. This openness is a symbol of God's love towards all creation. In the light of this open God we see that racism and sexism are idolatry, an idolatry that disfigures and destroys the quality of human life God intended for us to enjoy. The ecumenical God appreciates race and gender. We are invited to experience race and gender through this divine appreciation of them. We must not ascribe absolute value to our own race and gender. 'You shall have no other gods before me' (Exod. 20.3).

Idolatry creates a social power system which produces the human conditions that exist under the Brooklyn Bridge. Debilitating homelessness is created by human minds that are closed. The closed mind is loveless and therefore unfree. It is not an ecumenical mind. It is idolatrous. Jesus Christ is free from idolatry. Paul Tillich writes:

> And therefore the decisive story is the story in which he accepts the title 'Christ' when Peter offers it to him. He accepts it under the one condition that he has to go to Jerusalem to suffer and to die, which means to deny the idolatrous tendency even with respect to himself. This is at the same time the criterion of all other symbols, and it is the criterion to which every Christian church should subject itself.[1]

The Christ who goes to Jerusalem to suffer and to die is free of all possibility of idolatry. Where there is no idolatry, there is genuine freedom. It is this Christ who frees and saves us. This Christ embodies the spirit of the 'homeless/ecumenical God' who stands against the powers that dehumanize people and make them homeless. Again, let me quote from Manas Buthelezi:

> Christ's suffering on the cross, however, was redemptive; it effected the renewal of broken humanity. It was for the sake of others beyond the self, that is, it transcended the horizon of the sufferer. Through the cross God transformed the instrument of violence, vengeance and death into a vehicle of divine love and restoration to new life.[2]

God is transforming the instrument of violence into a vehicle of divine love. This is what we see as we live in this world today confessing faith in Christ. 'Lord, have mercy'.

Notes

1 Paul Tillich, *Theology of culture* (Galaxy, New York, 1964, p 67).

2 Manas Buthelezi, 'Some theological concerns raised by the unity/renewal study' in Stavanger (ed), *Faith and renewal: Commission on faith and order* (WCC, Geneva, 1985, p 181).

All bible quotes taken from the Revised Standard Version.

Evangelism, Mission and Evangelization

Albert Nolan

The richness of the Anglican theological heritage is that it brings together in one communion of Christians three theological traditions. The catholic, the evangelical and the ecumenical.

The catholic tradition has been handed down in the Anglican Communion from the centuries before the break with Rome, and still flourishes in the Anglican church not only in Anglo-Catholics, but in many others. I can feel and sense that tradition and the influence that it has had in the Church of the Province of South Africa (CPSA).

The evangelical tradition was born in the Anglican church one hundred and fifty to two hundred years ago, and it's very clear how much influence that evangelical tradition has had upon the CPSA. Then there is also the ecumenical tradition developed mostly by the World Council of Churches (WCC), with its emphasis upon justice, peace and the integrity of creation. That too has had an impact upon the thinking and the practice of Anglicans around the world and in Southern Africa.

Of course there are Anglicans who live out of only one or other of these traditions or who put a very special emphasis on one or other of these traditions. But the real richness of the Anglican tradition is the ability to combine the three and to benefit from the strengths of all three. Of course this is not always easy. It requires some clear theological analysis and reflection to do it effectively. Each of these three traditions has its strengths and its weaknesses. It is not possible for me to go into all three traditions in any great detail. I only want to touch on all three in relation to evangelism.

For the sake of simplicity, clarity and brevity for the evangelical tradition I want to focus simply upon the word 'evangelism' and its meaning. In the ecumenical tradition I'm going to look at the meaning of the word 'mission'. In the catholic tradition I want to focus on a fairly recent concept in Catholic circles: 'evangelization'.

The evangelical tradition: Evangelism

I would like to say that I have no doubts about the historical importance of the evangelical tradition and its continued importance today. Evangelicalism has had an influence, in one way or another, upon **all** Christians including those in the catholic and ecumenical traditions.

It has been the great campaigns of revival and evangelism during the nineteenth and twentieth centuries that has made Christianity once again a matter of choice and conviction rather than a matter of birth, ancestry and culture. In a world of nominal Christians with nominal beliefs, with faith that was a mere formality, it was above all evangelicals who challenged people to make a choice to accept Jesus as their personal saviour and to change their lives accordingly – to become 'born again' Christians. It is this particular way of preaching the gospel that we call evangelism.

While it is not difficult to see the value of this kind of revivalism, it is also not difficult for us today to see that evangelism is not everything. We have kept saying that. Evangelicals themselves, from the start nearly two hundred years ago, have always recognized the need for something more than just preaching and conversion. Discipleship, following in the footsteps of Jesus Christ, will include social action, social involvement and social justice.

This has always been part of the evangelical tradition, and whenever it has been neglected, as it has been by many evangelicals in South Africa, there have always been other evangelicals to bring them back to the true tradition: as was done, for example, by the authors of *Evangelical witness in South Africa*. The great strength, then, of the evangelical tradition and the particular value of emphasizing the need for evangelism, is that it reminds us of the indispensible need to preach Christ, and to challenge everyone to make a real choice for Christ.

This kind of preaching, however, should not be divorced from the preaching and practice of social justice as the evangelical tradition itself attests. Nevertheless, we all know that one of the major problems is precisely the modern use of evangelism to avoid social involvement and the questions of social justice. In practice there is a dichotomy for many Christians today between being 'born again' and working for social justice. We all know there should not be such a dichotomy, but in fact, it is the case.

Evangelism and social justice

So here is the theological problem we are faced with when we begin to think about evangelism today: what is the relationship between evangelism and social justice? Why do so many Christians think that you have to choose between the two? Why do we find it so difficult to hold the two together when we know that this is what we should be doing?

Perhaps we need to look beyond the evangelical tradition for an answer. It might be that Anglicans are in a particularly good position to do that. I haven't been able to find any coherent way, within the evangelical tradition, of seeing these two – evangelism and social justice – as one.

The ecumenical tradition: Mission

In the history of Christianity it has been above all, the role of the WCC to remind us of our mission to transform the world. It is true that this same emphasis can be found in the social encyclicals of the Roman Catholic Church, and even more so in the Third World theology of liberation. But it was the ecumenical theology of the WCC that developed a broad vision of the Christian churches as God's humble agents in transforming a world that abounded in almost insuperable problems: poverty, hunger, oppression, war, ideological conflict and environmental destructiveness. Faced with these massive world problems, and faced with a church that was irreconcilably divided about doctrine and teaching, and with the reality of other religions in the world it was the WCC that began to speak about the mission of Christian churches almost exclusively in terms of justice, peace and the integrity of creation.

Here again, we all needed to be reminded of this, especially in South Africa. The South African Council of Churches, particularly as it was led by Archbishop Desmond Tutu, brought the ecumenical dimension of the WCC to bear upon the situation in South Africa, and it has been extremely important for the history of Christianity here.

The church does not exist solely for the spiritual comfort of individuals nor solely to get individuals into heaven. We are also responsible for the earth, the world, the course that history will take in South Africa and elsewhere. The ecumenical tradition has forcefully reminded us of this again and again.

However, this mission of the church to transform the world should not be pursued without the equally important mission, the Great Commission to preach the gospel.

At first, there was something of a clash between these two traditions. Ecumenicals and evangelicals met in separate, and somewhat antagonistic, world councils and alliances. But, today this is changing. There have been very important meetings between ecumenicals and evangelicals for example in Stuttgart in March 1987. This meeting produced a very important statement about evangelism. It would not be true to say that the WCC had neglected evangelism before that; after all they had a department of mission and evangelism. But there were serious differences and the Stuttgart consultation enabled them to clear up some of these differences. I think that that was very important theologically.

The famous Stuttgart statement makes it clear that evangelism is absolutely necessary, that there must be 'an explicit invitation to each person to recognize and accept in a personal decision the saving Lordship of Christ'.

On the other hand the same document presents us with a number of cautions and I think these cautions may be of some value in the Decade of Evangelism. Here are some of them:

- evangelism should not be a simple telling, but a sensitive listening. If we're going to go around evangelizing the world, we must remember to listen to the world, to listen to people;

- the gospel is not a commodity to be advertized and sold like other commodities. The Stuttgart document speaks of its grave reservations about the use that is sometimes made of sensational radio and TV shows;

- evangelism is not only a matter of words. It also happens through the witness of a person's life and through the blood of the martyrs today. In some circumstances drama, music and art forms may be far more appropriate than words;

- we cannot export models of evangelism from one culture to another. The highly individualistic approach of the west in its evangelism is not appropriate or helpful in more communitarian cultures;

- there cannot be the same evangelism agenda for all churches everywhere. In other words don't just copy what has been successful in the United States for example. Let's find our own agenda;

- there is a need for an integral evangelism, an incarnational and contextual evangelism that integrates *kerygma* and *diakonia*, message and service, evangelism and mission.

One can sense something of the same concern and the same caution in the reports and resolutions of the 1988 Lambeth Conference, which initiated the Decade of Evangelism. While the Bishops called for a new determination to evangelize, that is to proclaim salvation through faith in Christ, they always add that what must be built no less painstakingly is the other aspect of mission: the relief of need, the revision of unjust structures of society, and the transformation of human existence.

This Lambeth Conference, as I understand it, brought together in an explicit way the evangelical and ecumenical traditions. There was a resolution about a Decade of Evangelism, but there was also a resolution, in the same conference, which called on Anglicans to participate in the WCC programme for Justice, Peace and the Integrity of Creation.

But in none of the Lambeth literature do I find a satisfactory theological account of how these two fit together. Everyone now seems to be convinced that we must have the two. But how do they fit together to form one whole?

It's for this reason that I want to turn to the catholic tradition. That's not just because I'm a Roman Catholic, but because I believe the tradition does have something to say in bringing together evangelism and social justice.

The Catholic tradition: Evangelization

Although the word 'evangelization' had been used before then, it was at the Synod of Bishops in Rome in 1974 that it really came into its own for Catholics. At that Synod and in the encyclical that followed, *Evangelii Nuntiandi,* or 'Evangelization in the modern world', the word 'evangelization' was used to cover all the activities, tasks and duties of the church. It was used to cover preaching and practice, word and sacrament (that was a big change for Catholics!) the personal and the social, salvation of the soul and political liberation. It was a sort of portmanteau word.

But it's not just a matter of words. The 1974 Synod used 'evangelization' to show that there is a unifying element in all that the church does (or should be doing), from preaching sermons to running schools and hospitals.

This is done with a concept of evangelization which is thoroughly biblical and which was worked out theologically, in the Synod and then in the Encyclical. It was defined as

> '. . . bringing the Good News into all the strata of humanity, and through its influence transforming humanity from within and making it new . . .
>
> It is a question not only of preaching the gospel in ever wider geographical areas or to ever greater numbers of people, but also of affecting and, as it were, upsetting, through the power of the gospel, humankind's criteria of judgement, determining values, determining

points of interests, lines of thought, sources of inspiration, models of life, which are in contrast with the word of God and the plan of salvation.'[1]

Evangelization is not exactly the same as evangelism. It includes evangelism, but it is clearly something much broader. Spreading the gospel of Jesus Christ includes the very important dimension of bringing individuals to personal conversion by preaching; but work for justice, the struggle for liberation, attempts to improve family life, campaigns against pollution, and liturgical services are all part of the process of evangelizing the world and we need to discover how they are all part of that one process.

Now, it's all very well to say that but we can also ask, if it is true, is it biblically based? I want to argue that it is. What we tend to overlook, I think, is that the Good News that we must preach and live is the Good News of the coming of God's realm – the reign of God – so that God's will may be done on earth as it is in heaven. Evangelization means working in every possible way, by preaching and by action to promote the coming of the realm of God.

Once we recognize that the core and the heart of the gospel is the kingdom, everything else falls into place. Calling people to a personal choice for Christ means calling them to a personal choice for the kingdom which Christ preached and initiated on earth. It means calling them to work, to struggle, to sacrifice, and to die for the coming of God's kingdom.

The gospel is about salvation from sin. But it is more than my personal salvation from my personal sins no matter how important that is. The salvation which Jesus preached was the coming of God's kingdom. In other words the salvation Jesus preached and that we read about throughout the Bible is not only about the salvation of souls. It is also about the salvation of bodies, the salvation of societies, and the salvation of our physical environment.

An unfortunate thing which has happened along the way in our Christian tradition is that the comprehensive meaning of the word salvation in the Bible, and as used by Jesus, has been narrowed down for many people to mean only the salvation of the soul, the individual. That has taken away from the tremendous value and richness of the message that we have been given. Let's look at this a little more closely.

Salvation

The soul

The salvation of the soul is of course extremely important. It is salvation from guilt; it means forgiveness. That kind of salvation is the forgiveness that we all need. Some people experience that need much more than others; I think it is an imposition to go around thinking that everyone experiences the need for forgiveness in the same way that we do. Not everybody does. But we do all need forgiveness.

The body

The salvation of the body – healing – is extremely important in the gospels. Jesus appears to spend more of his time healing bodies than saving souls. The word 'healing' is the same word as that for 'saving' or 'salvation' in Greek: *soteria*. So we must be very careful not to exclude the salvation of the body from the meaning of the word 'salvation'. It is part of God's activity in the world.

So, that means that anywhere in the world where we find healing, where we find people who are relieved of hunger, relieved of their sickness, sufferings, thirst, imprisonment and so forth, it is God's saving will. It is the Lord Jesus Christ moving again and again, no matter who does it. Let us remember that a crucial part of our belief, as Christians, is the resurrection of the body. There is no such thing as the salvation of the soul alone. We have to add the final salvation: the resurrection of the body.

Society

We in South Africa have become fully aware of what a social structure, a social system, can do to people, how evil it can be. No social system can sin, but through our sins we build social structures that certainly harm people. These are structures that we can call unjust and sinful. They also need to be redeemed and it is an illusion to think that we can do it individually. It is tempting to think that when every individual is redeemed then the structures will suddenly all change. But we need to look at structures themselves and think about their salvation, liberation or redemption.

Jesus did that. It is not without reason that when Jesus spoke about salvation he did so in social terms not in individualistic terms. He spoke about it as a new society: the kingdom of God. Now whatever else the word 'kingdom' may mean, it was in Jesus' time the word for a society, or nation. Jesus was talking about a community. Salvation meant a new community, a new society, a new universal nation: the kingdom of God.

This is where social justice comes in. Work for social justice is part of God's work of saving the world. It's not separate from salvation, it's not an optional extra. It's that part of God's saving work that is redeeming unjust structures, saving societies.

Nowhere in the Bible will you find that you simply have to do it one by one. We must convert individuals, but we must also try to change structures. They are all part of God's saving work.

Here, it becomes even clearer that we Christians must have the humility, when we see other people working for social justice and in fact succeeding, to look at that and say 'there is God at work'. To look at that and to be able to say that there is Jesus Christ the Risen Lord, influencing and saving our society, even if the people who do it are not committed Christians who have been 'born again'. God uses them anyway. The spirit moves where he (or she) wills.

So God's work of salvation also happens outside of the church. God is not bound by the rules and regulations of the Catholic church or the Anglican church. God works where God wants to. It is extremely important to recognise this. For one thing, it makes us realise that it is something of a scandal that many of us have been so little involved in trying to redeem or save society, or rather that God is not being able to use us, that we have been so concerned about our own salvation that often God has had to say 'these Christians, I'll have to go and find someone else to do it'. We need to be humbled and challenged by that. But, most of all, for our purposes of evangelization, we need to recognize that we haven't seen God's salvation broadly enough.

The environment

God's salvation extends beyond human society to the whole created universe which also needs to be saved and liberated. We all know the passage in Romans 8 where Paul says that the whole creation still retains the hope of being freed, like us, from its slavery to decadence or destruction, and to enjoy the same freedom and glory as the children of God (Rom. 8.19-21).

When I was a theological student we had enormous difficulty with that passage. How can you talk about the whole universe being saved? What is it to be saved from?

Today however, we know exactly what Paul was talking about. It has become very clear that our universe needs to be saved from our sins. It needs to be saved from the pollution of the atmosphere and rivers, the destruction of nature all over the world, the destruction of the ozone layer, the creation of the greenhouse effect, all these environmental issues that we read and hear about today. Now we see how the whole universe needs to be redeemed. Of course, we have people who are campaigning about it like the greens and the conservationists. But, as Christians, we need to be able to look at that and say that is the work of God. That is God using people, in this case to save the environment, for the sake of human beings. God has that concern even if you and I don't and is using those people for that purpose and it is part of God's salvation. Perhaps you're beginning to think that now I'm defining salvation so broadly that it really doesn't have much meaning left at all.

Salvation is always salvation from sin and I'm not trying to suggest that there's any kind of salvation that isn't, but sin has become far more comprehensive and widespread, at least in its consequences, than simply the private lives of people.

If we are going to be effective evangelists I think one of the very first things we are going to need to do in our preaching is to recover a deep sense of the pervasiveness of sin and the fact that sin is something that goes far beyond my soul. Sin affects us all. The sinner feels guilt but sin also affects other people. It's through my sins that other people are often sick, poor, hungry, homeless and thirsty. When I see poverty, I see Christ crucified, I see the results of sin. Similarly, with societies. If societies are corrupt and unjust it is because they have been penetrated by sin, the sins of the people who built them over the years.

An unjust society has everything to do with sin. If I talk about saving our society it must be precisely understood that I mean saving it from the result of sin. Similarly, with the pollution of the environment; it's because of sin that we have a problem with the ozone layer, it is because of the sin of greed, it is because people were not concerned about future human beings, it is because people are selfish and want to make money for themselves and cannot think of anybody else, that we have a problem with the ozone layer.

Even the ozone layer has something to do with sin, so if we talk about salvation and saving the ozone layer we're still talking about salvation from sin. Notice however, that we're not talking only about salvation from my sins, for me as a sinner. We are also talking about salvation from the consequences of sin, and about the need to be saved from being sinned against. The sins of apartheid and injustice need salvation for those who are sinned against. The Bible has many examples of this. Save us Lord from our enemies, save us from our foes, save us from those who hate us, save us from those who oppress us, that is salvation too: to be saved from the sins of others who sin against us.

Salvation is happening

There is a magnificent process of salvation happening in the world, maybe it's not enough but it is happening. It is God's work and it extends into every aspect of our lives, our society and our environment.

What would it mean to preach this form of salvation? I think that such evangelism would have two parts, in exactly the same way as Jesus' preaching of the Good News had two parts. For Jesus, the first part was announcing the coming of the kingdom of God. The second part of Jesus' message was always a call to repentance or conversion. I think first of all that evangelization today needs to have these two parts. In order to effectively announce the coming of God's kingdom it is necessary first to denounce the sins people commit in South Africa today. This would include the sins of racism, injustice, oppression, greed and the destruction of the environment. We must help people to understand the reality of sin and the dynamics of sin. They must realise that sin is thoroughly contextual.

So, first of all we need to do this, then we must proclaim from the rooftops that God saves us from sin. God is saving us from sin through Jesus Christ and it started many years ago with the birth of Jesus, with the life of Jesus, his death, his resurrection, and his ascension. It carries on today and will reach its climax in the second coming of Jesus in the coming of the kingdom on the last day. In other words, the events which we need to preach must be preached as a series of events. It must also be made clear that people today stand in the middle of these events. To put it another way, we are announcing the coming of God's kingdom, we are announcing where it began, in Jesus Christ and his life, death and resurrection, we are announcing that it is still going on today, and we are announcing that it is going to come to its climax in the future. We are in the middle of the events. This idea is extremely important if we are going to contextualize salvation. In announcing the kingdom it is also important to be able to see that God is doing a very broad work of salvation. The individual is being converted, but God is also interested in the salvation of the body, society and the environment. This will say to our audience, in our evangelism, there is hope that my sins can be forgiven: there is hope for our world: there is hope for South Africa: and there is hope for the environment. This is because of God and of what God did in Jesus Christ. I think that can come across as Good News.

The evangelical tradition has great value in connection with the second part of the message that we must proclaim. We must go on to say that all of us must become personally committed to Jesus Christ and to his message of the kingdom. We must live that. We must become more involved in God's plan for the whole world and for the total salvation of the world.

If we preach the gospel in something of this way my suggestion is that our evangelism will be fully integrated with our mission. It will all be the same work: for justice, preaching, and everything else, because we shall be able to see it all as part of God's great project to redeem the world and to establish God's reign on earth.

Note

1 *Evangelization in the modern world* (Papal Encyclical).

This essay is an edited transcript of Albert Nolan's address to the Diocese of Cape Town's Conference on Evangelism in Retreat in June 1990. It was originally published in the December 1990 issue of *Grapevine*, a publication of the Church of the Province of Southern Africa (Anglican). It is used here with permission.

The Cosmic Christ

K. H. Ting

The Cosmic Christ is a rich concept. It says something about Christ the meaning of which is quite beyond human understanding. We are only groping. It is a notion that has come to Christians who are no longer satisfied with the classical two-nature debate concerning Christ and want to make a shift. What I will try to do is present what we in China have in mind when we say fumblingly and clumsily that Christ is cosmic. To some Christians, to talk of the Cosmic Christ sounds like removing Christ to some celestial outer space. But this is actually not so.

The importance of context

In order to appreciate any proposition, it is important to know the particular circumstances under which it has come up and the particular problems it addresses. So let me describe to you the struggle in China in the course of which the notion of the Cosmic Christ has come to the fore on the part of more and more Christians. You will see that the notion is the result of the impact of historical changes upon inherited faith. The impact drives Christians back to the New Testament to meet the familiar words glistening with splendour and meaning as if for the first time. I am referring to passages on the person of Christ in, for instance, Colossians, Ephesians, Hebrews and John's Gospel.

The historical changes have been those since the birth of the People's Republic of China in 1949, which marked the beginning of a period of direct encounter between Christians and communist revolutionaries. In this direct encounter people, including Christians, were greatly impressed by the moral goodness which their new acquaintances, the revolutionaries, manifested and the goodness they could inspire in others. Their frugality, their self-sacrifice, their honesty in self-analysis, their relentlessness in dealing with corruption within their ranks, their programme for nation-building and their humility made them the incarnation of all that Confucius and other sages taught about the virtuous life. For instance, I knew of one Communist Party member who endorsed Paul's description of human nature as so often not doing what ought to be done, and doing exactly what ought not to be done. I understand some western Christians, equally impressed, went so far as to say that the new person spoken of by Paul had arrived, not in Christ but outside of Christ. The revolutionaries were the opposite of the caricatures of them meted out for popular consumption by the press under the previous regime. As a result, the writings of Marx, Engels, Lenin, Stalin and Chairman Mao became bestsellers.

Human nature being what it is, historical movements with high aims have a tendency to relapse and even to develop into their opposites unless there is constant, thoroughgoing criticism and self-analysis. With the gradual passing away of the revolutionaries of earlier generations, there has been a decline in revolutionary spirit and over-all moral standards. Bureaucracy and corruption have crept in. But let us not dismiss the spirit of dedication on the part of the revolutionaries, so many of whom are hard-working and self-giving even today. It is not a phenomenon of no consequence but one that makes Christians in China stop and think. It challenges us to find a good understanding and explanation from the point-of-view of our faith.

All along, Christian evangelism has capitalized on human depravity and lack of virtue as the entering point for preaching about sin and about Christ as Saviour. How are Christians to account for the new phenemenon which seems to make Christians' faith pale and superfluous?

Evangelism in a new context

The most catastrophic blow was on those Christians who knew and admired Jesus only as a great moral teacher, a social reformer and the leader of what some of them liked to refer to as the Christian Movement because of their dislike of the word 'church'. They considered the Sermon on the Mount as being the epitome of Christian faith. Their faith in their cause was shattered when they found that the Christians' programme for changing China was almost nothing compared to the large-scale and very impressive performance that the revolution had brought forth. For instance, opium-smoking and prostitution, which Christians had spoken against for a century, were done away with in a matter of months. In the mind of many people there lurked the belief that Christians only talked a lot, but that the communists put their words into practice. That notion was demoralizing to Christians. Thus, the fifties were years when many Chinese Christians were greatly bewildered. As Chinese, they welcomed the liberation and reforms it made possible but, as Christians, what were they to think was the *raison d'etre* of Christian faith? Quite a number left the church to join organizations considered to be more effective.

Segregation for some

But not all Christians were bewildered. There were hardliners who engaged themselves in the building up of a Great Wall against the inroads of new realities and new thinking. Their way of keeping themselves unmoved in their faith was to refuse to see any good outside Christianity. They thought nothing of the difference between justice and injustice, or between good and evil. The only divide they could see was the one between belief and unbelief. It was an even more negative version of Tertullian's 'What has Athens to do with Jerusalem?' They found their proof in 2 Corinthians 6.14-17 where it is said, 'Do not team up with unbelievers. . . . What agreement has the temple of God with idols? . . . Come away and leave them, separate yourselves, touch nothing unclean'. To them, God had lost the created world to Satan. The world had become Satan's occupied territory. Their proof was 1 John 5.19 which says, 'The whole world lies in the power of the evil one'. They used 2 Corinthians 11.14-15 to negate the beauty and goodness they saw around them: 'No wonder, Satan himself masquerades as angel of light, so it is easy enough for his agents to masquerade as agents of good'. Thus, as one preacher of that school wrote, God hates good even more than he does evil, because good is far more deceptive.

The practical implication of all of this was to shun anything of beauty in art and in nature, to write off any good human hands did and, meanwhile, to win the lost and wait for deliverance. With this world-view, Christians got comfort and strengthened their faith by looking for signs of the worsening of the human situation in the world. Some looked to the imminent return of Chiang Kai-shek's forces from Taiwan and the outbreak of the Third World War by which a vengeful God would, in his anger, bring about the annihilation of the world and the punishment of all unbelievers.

Many Chinese Christians found this kind of teaching unacceptable and politically dangerous. That teaching actually drove a good number of Christians to quit the church and 'join the revolution', as the saying went in those days. This kind of teaching dies hard. Today, many years after 1949, it still has a fluctuating market in China.

Many of the Christians who remained within the church seemed to hear the question Christ asked of the Twelve (John 6.67), 'Do you also want to leave?' They chose to answer like Peter, 'To whom shall we go? Your words are words of eternal life'. They began to bring the situation they were in to a renewed study of the Bible, fully conscious that 1949 marked a great shift in nation and perhaps in spirituality for Christians. Their former understanding of reality and truth needed to be deabsolutized so as to open a way for new insights and a new spirituality.

Christ as cosmic

For Chinese Christians the significance of knowing Christ as being of a cosmic nature lies essentially in ascertaining two things: Firstly, the universal extent of Christ's domain, concern and care, and secondly, the kind of love which we get a taste of in Jesus Christ as we read the gospels, love being the first and supreme attribute of God and basic to the structure and dynamic of the universe. In the light of this we get an insight as to how things go in the world. I will not try to take you into the world of Chinese classics, but will say that what they teach about the unity of the universe and the benevolence with which it is governed prepares the Chinese mind to treat favourably the preposition of a cosmic Christ.

Christ's work is universal

Christ's work, concern and care are universal. Christ is not so small as to concern himself only with religious, spiritual or ecclesiastical matters, or only with believers, or only with making converts of those who do not yet consciously believe in him. He is the one who sustains the universe by his word of power (Heb. 1.3). He has primacy over all creation. He existed before all things, and all things are held together in him (Col. 1.15,17).

It is not that God created the world, ceded its control to the successful rebellion of Satan, and then Christ came to rescue certain individuals out of it to be returned to God. As creativity is inexhaustible and creation a long process, Christ has everything to do with Creation thus far and with Creation as it goes on now. His concern is to bring Creation to its fruition, when love, justice and peace will become the rule. Redemption, like education and sanctification, does not stand against Creation but is one process with Creation. Not only communities of Christians here and there, but humankind as a whole and, indeed, the whole cosmos are within the realm of Christ's redemptive work. The Holy Spirit, in the same way, not only bestows gifts on Christians and the church, but also inspires all created beings with goodness and beauty.

Dealing with non-church values

The question as to how Christians are to think of non-church values, that is, values on the part of those who profess no faith in Christ, is, of course, not unique to mid-twentieth-century Chinese Christians. The first-century Christians faced it as soon as the gospel reached the non-Jewish world. Right at that point the church's process of discrimination, adaptation and assimilation began. In so far as China is concerned, the early Nestorian church had no hesitation in incorporating Chinese national culture, as shown by the fact that the 2,000-character inscription on the Nestorian Tablet uses the classical 'Book of Changes'. Matteo Ricci and James Legge were pioneers in bridge-building between Christianity and non-church values. It was unfortunate that the constructive missionary approach of both was invalidated in a fit of self-mutilating doctrinaire orthodoxy. The intransigent approach that ensued caused Christianity to mean alienation. The missionary approach in China consisted of divorcing converts from their heritage and from socio-political movements and protecting them with western colonial power. This led to a virtual collapse of Christianity with the success of the communist revolution in 1949.

Syncretism

My guess is that more or less the same story of alienation was repeated in other Third World countries. It seems that the depreciation of national cultures was particularly a vice of colonialism in its effort to justify itself. It was chauvinism and colonialism that was served when 'syncretism' was thrown around as an alarmist label. But the experience of human beings of different cultures living near to each other, brought about by modern technology and by the passing of colonialism, made the holding of nihilistic attitudes towards non-church goodness untenable. What is unusual about the experience of Chinese Christians in 1949 is that the breakthrough happened in a traumatic way, and that it was brought about by the challenge of a revolutionary movement under communist leadership.

We receive great consolation in reading Romans 5.15-17 where a comparison is made between the effect of Christ's grace and that of Adam's fall. Paul speaks of the infinitely greater impact of Christ on humanity than that of Adam by using such expressions as 'much more', 'vastly exceeded', 'in far greater measure', and 'out of all proportion'. We are elated and get a sense of liberation upon reading this. The Incarnation profoundly affects human and cosmic life in all its aspects. It is inconceivable that any area of human endeavour should be unaffected by grace. But too often, we make sin universal while limiting grace only to the few who profess a belief in Christ. It really amounts to saying that the Incarnation of the Son of God made less of an impact on humanity than the fall of Adam. But this is not a view which is consistent with a vision of God whose name is love and whose concern is to create, redeem, educate and sanctify a humanity that will reach perfection as free and intelligent agents or co-creators with him.

Atheism

Can we balance the existence of atheism with the idea of the cosmic role of Christ? I think we can, as much as we can balance the existence of many other things in the world with his cosmic role. In the first place, we have good reason to be grateful if we realize how much any denial of God or just the use of the term 'atheism' helps to bring up the question of God, and that this is an evangelistic service in any society which has little to suggest the idea of God. Also, atheists are not all of a kind. Some atheists only give consideration to what they can gain by assuming such a posture. There are rice atheists at least as much as there were rice Christians in the earlier days of Christianity in China. But there are other atheists whose cry against God is really a cry in favour of humanity. They are sincerely devoted to efforts to fashion a more humane society. Their atheism is not superficial but worthy of our sympathy. It is the rejection of the false notions of God that we religious people have put forward. The atheists' judgements can only be made on the basis of the ideas of God they come across, which usually are such distorted representations of the reality of God that atheists can hardly be expected to take that reality seriously. Who is the God they have in mind when they deny God's existence? It is the tyrannical Jupiter who chains Prometheus to a cliff because he does good for humanity, or the ruthless underworld King of Yen in Chinese popular religion who sends out emissaries to fetch people to be thrown into everlasting hell-fire as punishment for their demerits on earth. Atheistic humanism can be our ally as it can help greatly to salvage authentic faith. We can join forces with humanitarians in order to oppose the idolatry in those views of God that diminish human dignity and block human liberation. From our point-of-view, in the human pilgrimage towards the kingdom of God, we need not absolutise the opposition between theists and atheists. We both 'see in a mirror, dimly' (1 Cor. 13.12) while undergoing transformation into new persons in Christ.

Some of my friends are surprised that I sometimes speak as highly as I do of certain atheists and communists. What I want to say is that there is a part of me which utters a hearty 'Amen' to what they do and say, a part of me that refuses to rebuke them, but rather warms to them and wants to work together with them against forces we both want to combat, even though they and I have different objects of ultimate loyalty and get our orders from different chains of command. It is the conviction of many of my colleagues that, as long as there is space for Christian witness to be borne and for dialogue to be carried on, we must for the good of the church refrain from adopting confrontation and martyrdom as church policy.

To assert the cosmic dimension of Christ's role does not mean that everything that happens in nature and in history is Christ's work and design. Many things are happening that contradict God's loving-kindness and are harmful to the welfare of the world. Creation is a long process yet incomplete and, as Paul insists, imperfect and subject to frustration, especially as it involves the making of human beings who are not slaves but children of God. A world still in making must be one in which ugliness and devilry have their place. Events all over the world are telling us how tortuous the way is towards the perfect community of free, loving children of God, and how high a price in suffering God and human beings have to pay for every inch of progress towards that goal.

Unity in God

In the 19th century the picture that inspired many western Christians was that of the church going into the world and gathering all nations unto its fold. Today, what catches all Christians' vision is the picture of Christ leading the whole Creation towards the goal of unity in God. In this saving work of his, all human movements of progress, liberation, democracy and humanization are joined. The church is important as the place where Christ is explicitly known, confessed, adored and preached. The world needs the church's saving of forgiveness and reconciliation and peace. But God's saving work is not coterminous with the boundary of the church. It has the whole cosmos as its limit. As the Second Vatican Council has put it, 'Many elements of sanctification and truth are found outside the visible structure of the church and so the helps necessary for salvation are always and everywhere available to all who are obedient to the dictates of conscience'. I like to think that, if these elements are arcs of a circle, Christ is the perfect round in whom they will all be completed, fulfilled and united.

That the whole of reality is God's concern and Christ's domain seems to be a proposition already commonly accepted in western churches but, in China, we are still in the process of winning more Christians in order to see if this is true. We in China are reading in the Bible of how Abraham received blessing from Melchizedek, the pagan King of Salem, how Cyrus, King of Persia, a Gentile, carried out God's purpose and made possible the rebuilding of the holy city and the holy temple, how Nebuchadnezzer of Babylon also worked for God who thereby bestowed on him a recompense, and how, in Isaiah 19, God calls Egypt 'my people' and Assyria 'the work of my hands', alongside Israel 'my possession'. Because we have seen and experienced goodness, truth and holiness among followers of paths and ways other than those of the church, we cannot resist a vision of the universal creative and redemptive activity of God for all humankind, aside from the particular redemptive activity of God in the history of Israel and in the person and work of Jesus Christ. This is implied when we say that Christ is cosmic.

The other implication of discovering the cosmic dimension or nature of Christ is to ascertain love, the kind of love we get a glimpse of in Jesus' earthly life, as the supreme attribute of God and the principle by which the cosmos is run.

God is love

That God is love has become a platitude. We need to make Christ-like love the definition of God, the all-commanding part of the revelation of the nature of God himself. We have been trained to think of God mostly in terms of superior power which can either crush us or make us powerful. This is often a projection and legitimation of our power-hungry, exploitative, monopolistic social structures and attitudes. But in the New Testament, God's power is made perfect in weakness and God exercises sovereignty through the cross, not through conquest. We must stop fashioning God in the image of Egyptian, Persian, Roman and Chinese rulers, thereby giving to God the attributes which belong exclusively to Pharaoh, Caesar and their like. We need to put aside all those attributes such as God's absolute power, knowledge, changelessness, dominion and majesty, arbitrariness and intolerance, imposed on God but which reflect largely an absolutization of human beings (especially male human beings), own cravings. These attributes need to be deabsolutized and subordinated to God's supreme attribute of love.

That Christ is cosmic gives us assurance that God is the cosmic lover, not any cosmic tyrant or punisher. He works by education and persuasion rather than coercion and forced obedience. He lures and invites and waits for free response and does not resort to scolding and reprimanding. That is why many of us in China find the gospels' analogy of the transformation of seeds and the growth of plants in air, rain and sun more appealing than that of beating and controlling the sheep with rod and staff. God's is the will to fellowship, not the will to power. For Chinese Christians, to discard the image of a vengeful, frightening God, and to come to adore God the lover, the sympathizer, and the fellow-sufferer is a shift that is truly liberating.

During the so-called Cultural Revolution which turned out to be not only anti-cultural but also abusive of revolution as an honoured word, when injustice, hatred, thirst for power and arbitrary condemnation of the innocent ran riot, the image of God the Lover was seen to be such a shining contrast and source of comfort and hope that many were drawn to this God. He spoke lovingly to the heavy-laden and gave the unacceptable in the world an acceptability and rest they could not find elsewhere.

We need a different God, a God who loves as the cosmic lover with a love exemplified in Jesus Christ. We want to depart from the severe and intimidating God who is not the Christ-like God the four gospel writers want us to believe in. We like the image of God in Hosea (11.4) of one who secures us with reins, leads us with bonds of love, lifts us like a little child to the parent's cheek and bends down to feed us. To confess that Christ is God-like is now seen to be not so important as to affirm that God is Christ-like; and Christ-like love is the way God intends for the running of the cosmos.

God being love, more and more of us are seeing that the father figure is not necessarily the only or the best analogy for understanding him. For centuries and to this day, in China anyway, what is taken for granted in the father is his severity, and in the mother her loving-kindness. In fact, the proper Chinese way to refer to one's father in conversation is as 'the severe one in my family', while 'the loving one in my family' is reserved for the mother. There are Biblical passages which show no hesitation in using the image of the mother to indicate how God loves. In Isaiah 66.13, it is God who says, 'As a mother comforts her son, so shall I myself comfort you'. Again, in Isaiah 49.15, 'Can a woman forget the infant at her breast, or a mother the child of her womb? But should even these forget, I shall never forget you'. And in Psalm 131.2, the Psalmist says, 'I am calm and quiet like a weaned child clinging to its mother'.

Reality as becoming

This emphasis on God as the great lover working out his purpose for the world brings in its train an understanding of reality as becoming. It gives us hope for and beyond history. We cannot fathom the actual time and manner of the end of history but are sure that it will be the triumph of love and grace. The way from alpha to omega is never a straight line, but love accompanies the pilgrims. We have to go through tortuous ways, but we know how Christ says to us: 'A woman in labour is in pain because her time has come; but when her baby is born she forgets her anguish in her joy that a child has been born in the world'. We see the darkness that appears before dawn as well as the dawn that will surely arrive after darkness. As is so well said in Psalm 30.5, 'Tears may linger at nightfall, but rejoicing comes in the morning'.

The cosmic Christ and Chinese culture

These two points about Christ – the cosmic extent of his role and the Christ-like love with which God runs the universe – are not entirely foreign to Chinese culture. A passage in Lao Tze's *Tao Te Ching* says:

The supreme Tao, how it floods in every direction!
This way and that, there is no place where it does not go.
All things look to it for life, and it refuses none of them;
Yet when its work is accomplished it possesses nothing.
Clothing and nourishing all things, it does not lord it over them.
Since it asks for nothing from them,
It may be classed among things of low estate;
But since all things obey it without coercion,
It may be named supreme.
It does not arrogate greatness to itself,
And so fulfils its greatness.

This passage prepares the Chinese soil for receiving Christ whose dimensions are cosmic.

This text was originally given as an address by Bishop Ting to The Friends of the Church in China Conference at High Leigh in July 1991.

Learning from Sri Lanka

Tissa Balasuriya

An ambivalent task

Against the background of Sri Lanka it is difficult to talk of sharing the Good News of what God is doing today. First there is much suffering due to the ongoing violence of two insurrections during the past two decades. Many are living on the border line between life and death due to poverty, malnutrition, and unemployment. This situation is not due merely to short term factors, or to our own faults and follies in Sri Lanka. The foreign exploitation of nearly five centuries has added to our troubles and continues to do so.

The difficulty of talking about what God is doing is that those who call themselves Christians and God's chosen people have been very much part of the cause of the miseries of our people. If we assume that God is working through Christians the reply to the question of what God is doing today could be rather negative. Our consolation is in the consciousness that God is working through all persons and forces and that whatever is good comes from God's providence. In that sense all the efforts of our people to realize the values of love and sharing and community building can be spoken of as what God is doing today.

God presents us with a challenge to change the present unjust and sad reality of our lives. The hope for the future is in so far as many persons respond positively to the message of God, which Christians acknowledge as coming from the Lord Jesus through the scriptures and the church. Since I am writing in a Christian context I will refer more to what God seems to be doing today in relation to the churches. God is the God of justice and liberation, and invites Christians to follow sincerely the teaching of Jesus. A truly Christian response to this call would be good news for us.

Unfortunately the coming of Christianity to Sri Lanka has been seen very much as bad news for our people. The gospel of Jesus came with invaders who dominated our people for four and a half centuries. Even in the years since independence the so-called Christian countries have continued to collude with the big companies and the local élite in depriving many of a decent livelihood in a one world situation.

The good news for us however, is that there are some groups who are trying to remedy this situation.

Some gospel texts and the Jesus mission

Luke 4.16-19 and 28-30

In the tradition of the Old Testament prophets Jesus announced his mission as essentially a message of Good News to the poor, freedom for prisoners, the curing of the sick and the liberation of the oppressed. He said that the time had come when these were being realized. Jesus told the disciples of John the Baptist: 'Go back and tell John what you are hearing and seeing: the blind see . . . the Good News is proclaimed to the poor' (Matt. 11.4-5).

This key proclamation by Jesus was made on the sabbath in the synagogue of Nazareth where he was well known. The people were stunned, especially as he announced that this kingdom of God is not limited to Israel (verses 23-27). The people wanted to throw him down the cliff. They understood the radical revolutionary implications of his message.

Luke 6.20-38

This text presents the heart of the gospel of Jesus. The sufferings of the poor will disappear in so far as the kingdom of God is being realized. The poor in spirit, even if they be rich, would be detached from wealth. They would work for the realization of love and justice through sharing. They would then willingly share their wealth and the materially poor would thereby also be blessed. There would be no poverty and no inequality. If its values were truly accepted and lived, the coming of the kingdom of God would be a liberation and a blessing for all. This indicates a primary mission of the disciples of Jesus; a mission to the rich which would be totally different from the spirit of capitalism or the free market economy.

Verses 27-38 present the core evangelical call to love one's enemies. This love is to be expressed in action by doing good to those that hate you. This is much more than strict justice. Not only should we love our enemies and do good to them, we should not judge them because God will forgive us in the measure that we forgive others (verse 37).

This teaching is also in the 'Our Father', the unique prayer that Jesus taught his disciples. In it Jesus presents an intensely human-centred God, not an abstract philosophical concept.

Luke 11.1-4 The 'Our Father'[1]

In this prayer, Jesus honours God and then prays for the coming of God's kingdom. Thereafter he indicates two conditions for its realization; the ensuring of daily bread to everyone and the forgiveness of one another. This calls for a transformation of people and of social relationships. All will not have their daily bread without a major change in values, relationships and structures in society.

Matthew 25.31-44 The final judgment

From this text we can see some of the implications for the mission of the disciples of Jesus. There is no mention here of a church or religious organization being involved in the ultimate judgment of human beings. There is no reference to the sacraments as being necessary for salvation. The criterion of the final judgment is one's response to the needs of others. This criterion is applicable to all irrespective of their religious beliefs and practices. If this had been realized by Christians during the past five centuries, the story of the missions and the history of the world would have been totally different. Instead of exploitation by the powerful Christians there would have been love, dialogue, and sharing.

Mark 10.17-31

The story of the 'rich young man' gives a further confirmation of the exigencies of the teaching of Jesus. He does not dilute his message but challenges him to give up his wealth and follow him. This is a difficult call. 'It is much harder for a rich person to enter the kingdom of God than for a camel to go through the eye of a needle.' The disciples were shocked at these words.

Thus the priorities of Jesus are often quite different from those of the church. Christian mission has been thought of in terms of church membership and external sacramental practice rather than in terms of the love of God and of the needs of our neighbour. Thus mission has co-existed and even collaborated with colonialism and unjust economic systems. A consciousness of this now should lead Christians to a sense of repentance for the damage done both to Jesus and to our neighbour.

Jesus preached the kingdom of God

Jesus presented a radical new teaching, backed up by the witness of his life. He announced it as the 'kingdom of God'. Its central theme is the revelation of God as love. God loves us, understands us and fulfills us and in return we must love God and all human beings in God.

For Jesus, love has to be operative, effective and creative. Love bridges the gaps between people and builds solidarity and community. Love shares, is self-sacrificial and other-centred. In this sense love is radical; it does not compromise with injustice, corruption, waste or unconcern. It is active, tenacious and even ferocious when the loved one is in danger – as a mother when her child is endangered. Love never gives up.

Sin is the turning away from God, who is love. Love requires sharing; sin is selfishness, lovelessness, and untruthfulness. Jesus therefore opposed sin as contrary to the values of the rule of God on earth. Sin is both personal and societal, individual and communitarian. The kingdom of God is a situation in which sin, lovelessness, selfishness, untruth and injustice are overcome by love, mercy, truth and justice. It is right relationship between persons, among groups and to nature.

Jesus began a movement of human understanding, love and sharing rather than a mere organization of external religiosity. 'Not everyone who says to me, "Lord, Lord" shall enter the kingdom of heaven, but he who does the will of my Father who is in heaven' (Matt. 7.21). He dethroned the prevailing values of money, power, prestige and group selfishness. Instead he proposed sharing, service, love for the individual person and a universal human solidarity. His preaching thus relativised the authority of both civil rulers and religious leaders. God alone is the absolute. God's kingdom is a reversal of the usual conditions of society. The poor become rich (Luke 6.20), the first are last (Mark 10.31), the small become great (Matt. 18.4), the hungry are filled, the weary find rest, the mourners are comforted, the prisoners are freed, the lowly are exalted, the oppressed are liberated and those who lose their lives find them (Matt. 23, Mark 8.34, John 12.25).

The conversion Jesus wants

Jesus invited both individuals and society to a radical conversion to the values he proposed. He wanted to move people from:

Death	to	life, through death to self;
darkness	to	light;

error	to	truth and knowledge;
ignorance	to	awareness of self, others and God;
selfishness	to	unselfishness;
injustice	to	justice;
hatred and prejudice	to	love, including the love of enemies;
greed	to	sharing;
profit-seeking	to	need-serving;
pride	to	humility and service;
privilege	to	equality and empowerment of all;
abuse of power	to	service;
patriarchy	to	mutuality and partnership;
hierarchy	to	community and reciprocity;
domination	to	participation;
isolation	to	cooperation and communion;
indifference	to	caring and concern;
apathy	to	empathy, concern and commitment;
unfreedom	to	freedom;
hypocrisy	to	sincerity;
dishonesty	to	honesty;
duplicity	to	authenticity.

These pairs of words may not always express correctly the difference between good and evil. For instance, a woman's sense of service of others may sometimes be exploited by men and many women need to affirm, rather than efface themselves. Each pair of words needs to be clarified in order to be able to discern the virtue and evil in each of them.

The conversion Jesus wants is not from one religious organization to another, but from wrong to right relationships. This is both evangelical and acceptable to other religions.

Jesus, mission and evangelization

We can understand 'evangelization' to mean bearing witness to the 'evangelium', the Good News of Jesus. In this sense it would mean announcing the message of the rule of righteousness that Jesus preached. Thus understood evangelization aims at improving the other centredness in our society. It is a call for a greater humanity and self-realization among all, irrespective of particular religious affiliations. It means that each individual has a responsibility to value the message of truth, love, justice, freedom and peace, whatever the source of the message.

Thus non-Christians can evangelize Christians. The poor and the weak can manifest the demands of the gospel message to the rich and the powerful. Women can evangelize men concerning the sin of sexism and the virtues of mutuality. The laity can evangelize the clergy about the world and its demands. We can all evangelize one another by word and example.

The conversion of the nations does not necessarily mean conversion to a church, but to genuine humanity and the care of nature. The next stage of the kingdom mission has to be a worldwide endeavour for dignity and freedom from oppressive world systems and structures.

Jesus, kingdom and church

The church is a community historically linked to Jesus, seeking its motivation in Jesus, endeavouring to bear witness to Jesus and claiming its mission and organizational structure from Jesus. The church does not fully contain or exhaust Jesus. Jesus does not belong to the Church in such a way as to exclude others knowing and relating to Jesus. Jesus belongs to the whole of humanity, as do other great spiritual leaders of the world. Some in the church may not be of the kingdom; some in the kingdom may not be in the church.

In the kingdom of God as preached by Jesus there are
– no sacred persons; all humans are sacred; women and men
– no clergy; all receive the Holy Spirit
– no organization as such; no hierarchy; no patriarchy
– no exclusively sacred places, or times, no preferred race
– no privileged people of God; all places, times, people are of God and loved by God
– no unique book that excludes others; no special sacraments,
– no unique religion; no competition of religions.

The kingdom of God is prior to the church; it is the goal of the church, the criterion by which the church and its activities have to be determined and evaluated. A learning, reforming, transforming church can be an immense service to the kingdom, an example of communion and service to all. It can be a space of freedom especially for the suppressed, a champion of justice, a promoter of equality, a network of alliances for the poor and the weak. It must place its resources, goodwill and spiritual strength on the side of those struggling for the values of the kingdom of God whatever their religion. It would then be a home of holiness and active love for all.

A new paradigm of mission

The acceptance of the kingdom of God as the goal and purpose of the church would significantly change the church's theology, spirituality and mission priorities. Traditional missiology has seen the growth of the church, and service to the Christian community, as being the main objectives and priorities of mission. To change this would require a quantum leap in the whole life and work of the Christian communities.

Christians would have to be primarily concerned with the common good of all persons. The liturgy, catechesis, and pastoral action of the church too would have to be more human-centred, concerned with the life of the human community as a whole and of all people, Christian or not. The objective of the church would be the building of individuals and human community guided by the values of the kingdom: truth, freedom, equality, justice and peace.

This major paradigm shift in the life of individuals and of the church will require a change in the use of time and resources, of personnel and institutions. The formation of the clergy and of the laity would have to be radically altered in content, life style, method and evaluation processes.

What is God doing in Sri Lanka today?

In the 1930s and 1940s the churches in Sri Lanka lived the traditional theology and spirituality that they had inherited from previous centuries. There was a certain continuity in the concept of mission as there was no substantial change in the theologies of the churches during three or four centuries. The Protestants carried on the thinking of the Reformers, and the Catholics maintained the counter-reformation position of the Council of Trent.

Mission was understood as the effort to bring people to one's church, as the best means for the salvation of souls. Christians thought of themselves as divinely privileged. Mission was to be achieved by the implanting of the Church everywhere. Christians were organized in parishes with Sunday worship as the principal meeting point and occasion for catechesis. Christian schools and social services were the chief means of bearing witness to the faith.

There was an implicit alliance between the churches and the British, the colonial rulers. This alliance was quite clear in the case of the Anglican church as it was the established church of the colonial power. Christians were privileged under the foreign powers. A disproportionate number of Christians were employed in public services, thanks to the Christian educational system and imperial preference.

The churches therefore tended to depend on the foreign ruler for their rights, privileges and sense of security. As independence drew near, the churches were wary about their future under Ceylonese rulers. In the drafting of the constitution prior to independence Christians had a major say in including a safeguarding clause which stated that the Parliament of Ceylon could not pass any legislation that would be discriminatory against an ethnic or religious minority without a two thirds majority. There was also a right of appeal to the Privy Council in London.

The first major crises that the churches had to face after independence in 1948 were the restriction of the entry of foreign missionaries, the termination of the contract of the foreign nuns who had been working as nurses and the nationalization of private schools. Christians, especially Catholics, were deeply disturbed by these events.

For over one hundred and fifty years, since the end of the persecutions under the Dutch, the Catholics of Ceylon had sedulously built up their schools with great self-sacrifice. With independence, changes in the educational sphere were influenced by the nationalist and socialist movements. Significant sections of the Christian churches opposed the introduction of universal 'free education'. Christian leaders were also reluctant to support the switch to the vernacular medium of instruction. Their concern was that future generations would be handicapped by an ignorance of a world language. While the standard of English has deteriorated during the past three decades, there has been a tremendous revival in the national languages, Sinhala and Tamil, and in the arts and culture expressed through them.

In the mid-1950s and early 1960s the campaign for the national takeover of the schools was led by Buddhists and Hindus who felt that the religious education of their children was neglected in Christian schools. Christian schools were viewed as agencies for proselytizing children into becoming Christians. At that time the churches refused to teach other religions in Christian schools, as these religions were regarded as false. Christians were perceived as having a social advantage over others because of the better facilities in their schools and therefore socialists and Marxists also supported the takeover of the schools.

Through this whole process the churches have had to find their place in a country now ruled by Sri Lankans, the majority of whom are Buddhists and Hindus. This has helped to make the churches less institutionalized and more open to social change. They are now open to teaching all religions in their schools, as the entire theological climate concerning inter-religious relations has changed at world level. In recent years however, a fundamentalist trend seems to be coming in with the new Christian sects and their intense, salvation-oriented propaganda.

Lessons we are being taught

The historical experience of the past fifty years has been teaching us some valuable lessons. The Spirit of God, operating through historical events and movements, has made us conscious of things that we were not aware of before.

We realized that Christians and theology have to **return to Jesus** and the core of the gospels. These were neglected or bypassed by historical Christianity. Christians have been preoccupied with building the church and have neglected the values of the kingdom of God as preached by Jesus. We have to rethink the mission of the church as being the fostering of genuine love and right relationships among people and communities at all levels. Redemption is in the restoring of love and mutuality among all people, communities and with nature. Who then are the missionaries?

In order for the objective of God's mission to be realized in our context of poverty and social injustice, there has to be an effort to bring about love and sharing in society. For this we have to **analyze and discern our society**, the social forces that are operative here, and join hands with those who are for justice and human understanding. This requires a struggle against oppression.

The Sri Lankan situation of continuing internecine violence is leading us to appreciate the **value of peace** and the need to care for human life. The vicious circle of poverty, discrimination, hatred, revolt, death and destruction is teaching us many lessons on the tasks and priorities of mission. Our earlier neglect of social and ethnic issues contributed towards bringing about a situation in which we became helpless before the organized violence of the militant groups and the State.

Our experience has taught us many lessons concerning the **nature and limits of religion**. We now see that the Christian claim to be the unique and exclusive path to salvation and holiness has been counter-productive. It not only prevented us from seeing the good in others, it also made us suspect in the eyes of others. We now acknowledge the salvific and liberative potential in other religions, as well as recognizing the religiosity sometimes expressed through folk religions. The growth of secular thinking and the relative failure of religions to bring about peace with justice in our country has shown us that religions too have their limitations and even enslaving features. Despite these limitations, the core values of religions are seen as the inspiration for rebuilding our country. Inter-religious relations and inter-Christian ecumenism are now accepted as normal in the life of the churches.

The two ongoing insurrections since 1971 are indicating to us the importance of **justice in social as well as ethnic relations**. Employment, language, culture, religion, lands and a homeland are extremely important issues in the life of people. National sentiments can be hurt and roused to the extent of civil war and young people are particularly susceptible to such influences. Christians have to give justice a top priority as right relations and life itself depends on it.

As elsewhere, we have become more conscious of the exploitation of **women** during the past two decades. In the poor countries of Asia the burden of women is even greater than elsewhere. In addition to exploitation within the home, they are cheap labour for the feudal and capitalist enterprises, migrant workers in foreign countries without human rights, and prostitutes due to poverty both at here and abroad. The recent tragedy of the million Asian migrant workers in Kuwait and Iraq mainly involved women. We are also being made aware of the cruel exploitation of children, especially as child labour and, to some extent, as child prostitutes. In the Sri Lankan context, all these are connected with social injustice.

Mission has to do with human life; the rapid despoiling of **nature** is now bringing to our attention the fact that we need it for our sustenance. Care for the environment, for the top-soil, for the forests, animal and plant species and for the waters and the seas needs to be given a higher priority than hitherto.

The Sri Lankan experience of **socio-economic policies** during the past two decades has shown us that both the socialist approach from 1970-1977 and the uncritical openness to capitalism since 1977 have not benefited the country. We have to seek a viable alternative that safeguards our national interests and brings about social justice while being open to modernity and new technologies.

Our troubles of the past two decades are also teaching us that what happens in society affects the life of the churches. At least out of self-interest, we Christians must take an active interest in wider society. The traditional ways of ministry however, are not adequate. The situation seems to be calling us towards a **reshaping of the traditional ministries of the church** such as the eucharistic liturgy, catechesis, parish education and social services. Priestly, religious and laity training has to be developed to form church workers for present day needs.

Basic human groups committed to core values are needed especially in our plural societies. Whereas basic Christian groups can be formed in 'majority Christian' countries, in Sri Lanka it is more appropriate to form action groups according to the people's interests and commitments. People committed to justice and peace are found in all religious and other groups. The essential requirement is that a person endeavours to transcend the limits of gender, ethnic group, religion or social class in order to serve the wider community.

Some priorities for the 1990s

- Ensuring ethnic harmony and the devolution of power.
- The protection of human life and human rights.
- The development of democracy, and the safeguarding of free elections, and a free press.
- The safeguarding of the unity and integrity of the country as well as the rights of religious and ethnic communities.
- Justice and equality to women who are, at the moment, exploited at home, in the workplace, in religions, and abroad as migrant workers.
- Balanced economic growth with social and ethnic justice.
- Concern for the transcendental value of all persons and the core values of freedom, dignity, equality, truth and justice.

Christian mission in Britain today

From this reflection on gospel texts and on the Sri Lankan experience some comments may be offered concerning evangelism in Britain in the coming decade.

First of all some rethinking is required concerning the **understanding of Christianity in Britain** over the past centuries. In Britain too there has been a misunderstanding of the core message of Jesus. The accent has been on building the church rather than on building human community on the values of the kingdom. There has been too close an alliance between the church and the state. This is particularly true of the Anglican Church, which has been called 'the Tory Party at prayer'. The dominant theology and missiology has tolerated the compromise of the churches with capitalism and colonial enterprise. Both these are, however, motivated by values that are incompatible with the gospel of Jesus.

From this would follow a question about **how Britain accumulated its wealth** over the centuries. To what extent was it the result of the exploitation of colonial people, piracy, the removal of treasures, and the misuse of power? The terms of trade were unfair and deprived the colonies of the fruit of their labour and the value of their raw materials. Whole populations were transferred as slaves or indentured labour to other countries. What is their present position, and what has been the impact on the receiving countries? Is there a duty of compensation to the victims in such situations?

The present **world economic system** is grossly unfavourable to the poorer countries, and benefits richer countries like Britain. It is a deadly system that brings about the death of many who are too poor to buy the food they need for living. It is a **killer system**. Some of its characteristics raise issues of public morality.

- There is no effective check on the large multinational companies that exercise total control on the prices of raw materials and produced goods. They are not accountable to any authority that ensures the just demands of the poor. The so-called free market system favours the already wealthy, as money determines the use of resources. They buy the support of local élites and rulers in the poor countries and they conspire to install regimes that will support them.

- The debts of Third World countries have led to a situation in which there is a net outflow of funds from the poor to the rich countries. The people of goodwill in the creditor countries are powerless to change this demand for total repayment.

- The gap between the poor and the rich is growing both within and among countries. Poverty within Britain has been growing during the past decade, with continuing unemployment, homelessness, drugs, crime and violence, especially in the inner cities. The helplessness of the people of good-will in Britain before the power of social forces like government and big business may enable them to understand, to some extent, the nature of the problems in the poor countries.

- The arms trade, including that in Britain, is a waste of valuable resources, a misdirection of research and a cause of conflict and destruction in the poor countries.

- Agencies such as the International Monetary Fund and the World Bank impose conditions on the poor countries that make their economic conditions worse. Rich countries, who have a major share in their decision-making, do not permit the reform of the agencies for the benefit of the poor. An immense international effort would be required for this.

The **world political system**[2] and concept of international law are assumed to be just, but they perpetuate the imbalanced division of land that was determined by colonialism. The world political system does not give a fair deal to the poor countries. Britain was largely responsible for setting up this world order through the British Empire but British public opinion and the churches in Britain have not been very articulate on this gravely unjust issue.

Britain is increasingly entering the **European community**. We welcome this coming together of nations but many questions arise as to what values will motivate this new superpower that is being generated.

The **transformation of the Soviet Union** and the collapse of socialism in **Eastern Europe** have generated an understandable sense of euphoria in the capitalist world. The churches too have emerged as survivors and winners after a long period of persecution and marginalization. These changes are to be welcomed but we must also be conscious that capitalism is the principle motivating spirit of the world system. It is that same world system that condemns so many to death and to a meaningless existence in the poor countries. It would be a pity if the changes in Eastern Europe lead to an incorporation of those countries into the exploitative capitalist system.

The **life style** of the affluent is one which the world's shrinking resources cannot bear. Britain can take substantial credit for building up the modern system of industrial economy, but we have now come to a position in which this pattern of industry cannot continue for long without grave damage to the environment. The non-renewable resources are being exhausted and this is leading to competition for their control. The **care of nature** has to be a major concern of public policy and education in the future.

The **multi-racial** and **multi-religious** character of Britain issues the challenge to transcend one's narrowness. The Congress of Black Catholics in Britain held in London in 1990 pinpointed many areas of racial discrimination. If people of other racial groups and religions are to be accepted as having rights of full citizenship then deep changes will be called for in the mind-set and spirituality of the average British person.

Spirituality is at the heart of all these issues. Do we as humans acknowledge the equal rights of others to life, liberty and leisure? Can we identify with the others as children of God? This is the basic call of the Jesus message.

Responding to this challenge as conscious Christians, the people of Britain can grow spiritually and thus help fulfill God's liberating purposes for all. A due concern for others is essential for one's own fulfilment. Those who take an excessive share of the earth's resources and thereby deprive others of the bare necessities of life, cannot be content with themselves or be sincere Christians. They would be like the rich man Jesus speaks of in the gospel. The challenge for British Christians, as for all of us, is not to worship the idols of money, power and privilege. Mammon is the name Jesus gave for this idol. We cannot serve God and Mammon.

Unremitting work

God's action in our societies is to invite us to work unremittingly for new relationships individually, in community and with nature. For this we need a serious and sincere analysis of our personal values and social structures. We must try to discern what God is telling us through the social forces and movements of our time, be they religious or otherwise.

Strategies for bringing about such change is a major difficulty for all groups because of the tendency for humans to look after their own self-interest. The world situation demands a restraint in consumption and a sharing of wealth and power. This task is all the more difficult for church-related groups because of the ongoing decrease in the numbers who participate in church-related activities. The 'unchurched' are a large proportion of the British population, although Britain is considered to be a Christian country. All the same, the call of the gospel is gradually leading to significant changes in the liturgy, catechesis, and pastoral activity of the churches. The spread of a theology related to human liberation is a contribution in this direction.

The human struggle for life, survival and human dignity is common to all countries. The disciples of Jesus are called upon to take their place alongside that struggle, for the action of God in history is through such processes. Our mission is to contribute to the redemption of persons, society and nature by establishing right relationships among them. In the process, like Jesus, we will have to suffer much. God's action in Britain will then be more clearly seen. As Jesus commanded 'love one another, just as I have loved you' (John 15.12).

Notes

1 Tissa Balasuriya, *Eucharist and human liberation.* (SCM Press, London/Orbis Books, New York, 1977, chapter 12.)

2 cf. Tissa Balasuriya, *Planetary theology.* (SCM Press, London/Orbis Books, New York, 1984, chapter 2.)

Stumbling-block, Folly, Good News

John S. Pobee

My context

It is a truism that our backgrounds shape us and determine to some extent our perceptions and misperceptions. So permit me to begin by declaring from whencc I come. First I am an Anglican with roots going back through my mother to the first African Anglican clergyman, Rev. Philip Quaque, who was the son of Cabosheer Cudjoe and was ordained 'missionary, catechist and schoolmaster' in the service of the Society for the Propagation of the Gospel in 1765 and ministered in the Gold Coast until his death in 1816. The Anglican tradition has been in my genes, so to speak, and my continuance in it is a kind of 'apostolic succession', though not in the technical sense. The Anglican style of *via media* is part of my heritage and style. What am I doing when as an Anglican I prosecute mission? Is it to recruit for *Ecclesia Anglicana*? Is becoming an Anglican the test of success in mission? And what, at any rate, is the value of being Anglican, when we engage in mission as Anglicans? In any case what value may we attach to the *Ecclesia Anglicana*'s character as church 'by law established' when we talk of missions? Second, I have never really known poverty or riches. My family was influential but not rich. In my lifetime the family influence has been because of a tradition of and involvement in education at home and abroad. I affirm God's **preferential** option for the poor, but I cannot speak for the poor because I have not known poverty. I affirm various critiques of the rich but I am unable to be violently anti-rich because I have never been in their shoes.

I come from what has come to be known as the South, sometimes also called developing or underdeveloped nations or the Third World. Such terminology annoys many. Let me say I use none of these expressions in a perjorative sense. I use them only as shorthand for a large world which is marked by two or three things. It is the laboratory and crucible of tremendous and horrendous tragedy. Missions herein are crying for liberation, the peoples are concerned to free themselves from oppression, slavery, poverty and hunger; the majority are illiterate. Here too certain questions press themselves on us. Has mission anything to do with this poverty and the yearning for liberation? What is the nature of mission in such a context? Even if, as Pope Paul 6th said 'the new name for peace is development', is mission just another form of welfare work? The fact is several churches in Africa, in the name of mission, have become just another development agency and perhaps lost the cutting edge of mission. Yet many are also marked by an infectious joy which makes them the envy of the rich and the individualistic. And yet, again, it is here that Christianity has found its centre of gravity, with the church growing fastest and being most alive[1] at the same time as other religions like Islam are growing. To this we shall return in a little while. But this last background of mine, together with the previous two, influence my understanding of the gospel and of the mission of the people of God. That is why I have called this article: Stumbling-block, folly, Good News.

The message of mission is the message of the cross: Folly, stumbling-block, God's wisdom

The title is a paraphrase of 1 Corinthians 1.18-24. There we learn that the central message of the earliest community of believers was 'Christ nailed to the cross' (1 Cor. 1.23; 2.2; cf. Babylonian Talmud Sanhedrin 43a). The cross was the heart of the gospel and many in the history of the church were to experience crucifixion and other types of persecution (Tacitus, *Annales* 15.33; Josephus *Antiquities* 18.63-64; Eusebius *Historia Ecclesiastica* I.II. 7-8). Many have come to experience and know the cross; many have come to know the meaning of the cross through other experience. Can it be a surprise that the cross was the heart of the gospel? Can it be a surprise that it is the poor, those who suffer and those who are marginalised who have welcomed in a deeper way the word of the cross? Africans came to know the cross in their situation of misery. We have come to see the cross of Jesus Christ as the cross of the South, thus carrying within ourselves the hidden Christ.

Be that as it may, beyond the historical fact, Paul adds an interpretation, which is three fold: first, Christ was nailed to the cross for us or for our sake or for our sins. It is interpreted as an expensive vicarious sacrifice and reparation for the sins of humanity. I have elsewhere[2] argued that it is through the martyr-theology of late Judaism that such a positive interpretation could be given to what, by all accounts, was a disaster. Here we locate the mystery of the Good News: the seeming disaster, folly or offence turns out to be Good News. Of course, we dare not forget the resurrection. But in my view the crucifixion and the resurrection are two sides of the same coin. In that complex, the cross is the symbol of **love** which announces that **love victorious overcomes evil.**

A word more about the poverty and misery of the South. This illustrates in vivid terms what sin is and how it is structured in history. Sin is structured in injustices and in the corruption of everyday life and experience; it is made evident in the heartlessness we experience everyday. Sin is a reality and hangs thick on humanity. The message of the Good News of the cross is about liberation from sin. But it is also a symbol of human sin that would kill even the just and good person.

The second comment Paul makes is that the crucifixion of Jesus was a stumbling block (Greek: *Skandalon* – offence)[3] to the Jews. Third, the message of the crucifixion of Christ was folly (Greek: *moria*)[4] to the Greeks. Let me dwell a little longer on the last two interpretations of the word of the cross.

For the Jews hanging was not only painful (Philo, *Flacc.* 72; Midrash Tehillim 11.7) but also a shame and a curse (cf. Deut. 21.23). Indeed, it was a sure sign that whoever so suffered was rejected of God. Therefore, to make the crucified Jesus the heart of the Christian proclamation was to make a scandal, to create a stumbling-block to faith in the holy and good God. Besides, divinity that can be subjected to crucifixion could not, by natural reasoning, be serious God. And here precisely is the irony and mystery so characteristic of God's ways: the transcendence of God which is often found in the least expected places and ways. This will be picked up later. For the present let me emphasize that mission that is devoid of the mystery of God is not mission. Mission is to attest to the mystery of and in life. I put it this way to emphasize that religion is ultimately an exercise in finding answers to the mystery of life and therefore, whatever else we do, it must be earthed.

For the Greeks, crucifixion was the 'most cruel and terrible penalty' (Cicero, *In Verr* 2.64; 5.64) reserved for slaves (Tacitus, *Annales* 4 3,11), hardened criminals, deserters and persons guilty of high treason and insurrection. There is yet another reason why the message of the cross was foolishness to the Greeks: it was a scandal of particularity – how could any person in their right sense fasten onto the cross as the turning point in the history of salvation, especially in a world which had a cyclic view of history? How on earth does any sober-minded person fasten on to the obvious disaster of the cross as the key to salvation? Obvious folly! But it is God's unsearchable wisdom – a mystery of faith. Mission is to share with others the mystery of faith which by normal human reckoning is folly. It is to share irony, so characteristic of God's ways of dealing with humanity.

Some deductions

Mission as proclamation of God's mystery

Be that as it may, certain deductions can be made from this mystery of faith. First, to be a missionary is to be a messenger of the mystery of God and a fool for Christ's sake (1 Cor. 4.10). For at the heart of the message is the seeming contradiction which is the mystery of the gospel and the mystery of God. This demands that spirituality shall be the dynamo of all authentic mission. Whoever would bear the mystery of God to the world must first be initiated into the mystery of heaven to see and hear what is going on there and to bear testimony of it to others. Seeing and hearing, like the prophets of old did, and obeying what is seen and heard are marks of that spirituality. It is only when you see the marks of the nails in the hands of Jesus, that you can see and experience Christ and be emboldened to go and tell the story to others. Mission is also to pray; to be responsive in God's name to the temporal life. Without spirituality mission can become just a crusade which could obscure the mystery which alone transforms folly into Good News and hope.

Of course, the word spirituality is often suspect. There are, no doubt, some dangers such as reducing prayer to a political act, or even the development of the spirituality of paternalism/maternalism or of privileged guilt.[5] In my view spirituality is about salvation which itself is about temporal liberation and yet more – a new human being, a heart cleansed from all sin, a new person who does not speak with animosity in her/his heart, who does not further violence, hatred or rancour (cf. Gal. 3.26-29). It is also about transcendence. It is a pilgrimage to eternity with a commitment to redeeming the here and now for the God who created the whole world. That message of the cross is the transcendental passage. This is what gives the church its originality, which no other promise of liberation seems to possess.

Precisely because of the dense fog around the word spirituality, let me cut a long discussion short by approvingly quoting the definition of the Indian lay theologian and ecumenist, M.M. Thomas. Spirituality is 'the structure of ultimate meaning and sacredness within which men (sic) may live and enter into a relationship with nature and with fellow men (sic)', in politics, economics, society and culture. And he adds: 'the primary concern of the Christian Mission is also with the salvation of human spirituality, with man's (sic) right choices in the realm of self-transcendance, and with structures of ultimate meaning and sacredness – not in any pietistic or individualistic isolation, but related to and expressed within the material, social and cultural revolution of our times. The secular strivings for fuller human life should be placed and interpreted in their real relation to the ultimate meaning and fulfilment of human life revealed in the divine humanity of the crucified and risen Christ'.[6]

Let me add three points to what is said of spirituality. Spirituality is based on trust in God. But we know that some people, particularly in the North, have difficulty in praying, in speaking to God and in speaking about God. We need to work on this spiritual crisis if spirituality is truly to become the dynamo of mission. Again, social relations based on love and justice are evidences of spirituality. Further, spiritual life includes a sense of identity which means a *metanoia* (i.e. repentance and conversion) from alienation to true humanness.

Folly of martyrdom and mission

A second consequence of initiation into the mystery of God is persecution and martyrdom. To dare to proclaim what one has seen and heard in the heavenly court, the mystery of God, is often to stand *contra mundum* and to pay the price for that stand and to experience the cross of Christ, whether as a confessor or as a martyr. Zeal for the Lord expressed in mission makes one look foolish and suicidal because one represents an unpopular opinion, becoming a displeasure to those who have privilege and economic power, in fidelity to Christ. Mission is self-surrender to the creator God even unto suffering and death. And how many have been renewed by such seeming folly which leads to suffering! It has been true to say that 'the blood of the martyrs, that is the seed of the Church'. To be as a fool, to bear one's cross in the name of Christ, is to lead people to the eschatological vision in which God is sovereign and omnipotent and thus to lead them to renewal.

Let me attempt to illustrate this point in two ways. First is the story of Elijah. His prophetic career was during the rule of Ahab, son of Omri, King of Israel and his wife Jezebel, the daughter of King Ethbaal of Sidon. Through her, despotic rule and foreign cults were introduced into Israel, thus undermining Israel's tradition and religion. The prophet Elijah took them on as a zealot for the Lord, leading up to the slaughter of the prophets of Baal at Mount Carmel. By the standards of the world Elijah was a fool to take on the powerful Jezebel who was sure to seek revenge. Of course, all too soon reality struck home and Elijah fled. He become a fool for the sake of God. Yet by that 'dare-devil' stance, he upheld the word of God in the land. His was a mission which by all human standards was folly but was God's instrument for 'hallowing the name of the Lord' and it was a witness to God through suffering.

The other illustration is a more recent one, from the life and work of Archbishop Oscar Romero (1917-1980), the famous Roman Catholic Archbishop of San Salvador who was assassinated in 1980 while saying Mass. He shepherded a church that had become a thorn in the flesh of the right-wing government of El Salvador. The government had in turn subjected that church to persecution and slander on the pretext that the church was being subversive and communist. But the church had only been trying to live its vocation of fidelity, its God-given mission of denouncing in no uncertain terms the sins of a society which held many in excruciating captivity and also called for a more just and humane society. That is their contemporary version of the mission of Christ. On the other hand, the experience of suffering arising out of their fidelity to mission, far from destroying them, created a sense of solidarity and unity. Let us now leave the Archbishop to speak for himself: 'This unity and solidarity is for me a very clear sign that we have chosen the right road. But the events of the last months [persecution] remind us that the union of Christians is obtained not by lips confessing a single faith but by putting that faith into practice; it is achieved around effort, a single mission. It is obtained in faithfulness to the word and the demands of Jesus Christ, and it is built upon common suffering. There can be no unity in the Church while the reality of the world we live in is ignored'.[7] To put it in other words, to be faithful to God's mission is to realize in oneself the cross of Christ, the acme of persecution. That is folly. But it is God's way of redeeming the world. To confess the cross is to bear the cross in yourself. The Decade of Evangelism will be nothing until we experience the cross in ourselves. One more quotation from Romero: 'The church must echo their [i.e. the suffering people's] anguish. . . . If we want to be a church that responds to the people's sufferings, we must make their cries our own. If we do not, we are not giving all the response that God wants to give to those who suffer'.[8]

Transvaluation of values

The third deduction from the folly of the cross is that mission is the transvaluation of values. What is folly or scandal becomes God's wisdom for salvation. This transvaluation of values runs through the gospel story and the history of mission. Thus the saviour is not born in a palace; he is born in a stable. What a rebuke for our love for establishment and privilege and position! Salvation is not only by dazzling acts of miracle, but also by the despicable cross which is heaven (John 12.20-26). The Good News affirms me as an African but also challenges me to 'press toward the goal to win the prize which is God's call to the life above, in Jesus Christ' (Phil. 3.14). I do not have to become as a European or Anglican in order to be a Christian[9]; more important is that I may be renewed in Christ as an African. How misguided some missionary practices have been! The message of the cross is Good News of a new humanity which is meta-cultural, trans-national and trans-denominational, because all natural identities have been transformed, transvalued and have become the solvent of the one gospel of the cross. Mission renews and its test is whether it renews humanity in God's image or not. Its test is not whether you become as a European, whatever value you put on that: What a rebuke to the commonly used comparison between Christian mission and European civilization!

The irony of the cross is these days much expressed in terms of God's *preferential* option for the poor. Through the experiences of the people of the South, we have discovered anew that Christ in his ministry had a preference for the poor and the known sinners; prostitutes, tax-collectors, lepers, Samaritans and outcasts. The follies and scandals of society were sought out by Christ. And we have learnt that in encounter with such as these, the people of God find the most pressing need for conversion (cf. John 3.17). We are also learning more and more that on the basis of Scripture, especially on the basis of the irony and mystery of the cross, the élite who question their self-understanding and perspective of élitism and learn from the poor, seeking to live their faith in living contact with the poor, will experience anew the joy of the Spirit at the foot of the cross. Mission from the perspective of God's preferential option for the poor is the proclamation by word and deed, and under God's grace, that enables people, especially the rich, to acknowledge what rightly belongs to the poor. This perspective invites the rich to repentance and is thus Good News, offering them a praxis and a future beyond the contemporary injustice which keeps nations in captivity.

Significance of stumbling block, folly and Good News

Stumbling block, folly and Good News – that is the message of mission. What is the significance of this? To affirm that the cross is heaven (John 12.32) is to proclaim that it is the hope of the world. The story of the cross proclaims that in the final analysis, empirically, sociologically, religiously and theologically, the forces of evil and power do not have the final word (cf. Rev. 7.15-17). The cross has become the symbol of the power of truth over the forces of oppression. That is the ground of hope and the Good News. It has been verified time and again in world history. The crucified carpenter from Nazareth, after some two thousand years, continues to exercise enduring moral influence in the world. The Pope who commands no legions apparently has more enduring influence than the politically and militarily mighty. The all-powerful USA was defeated in insignificant Vietnam and the all-powerful USSR was beaten by the relatively weak and not too-well organized Afghanistan freedom-fighters. Powerful dictators in Africa and powerful ruthless systems around the globe have been collapsing before less equipped freedom-fighters, often armed with moral strength and righteous indignation. Nkrumah of Ghana, Amin of Uganda, Tombolbaye of Chad, have fallen, in spite of their command of mighty resources. Colonialism has collapsed; apartheid is tottering. Therefore the forces of evil and power do not in the final analysis have the last word. We know that in all the struggles, religion has been a factor. Hope does not come from might or force. That is the insight of the seeming foolish message of the cross. But how do we join God to make this a real experience for the world today? That in essence is mission for today.

An aspect of this point about the final defeat of the forces of evil is that evil and good are never too far apart. It was Alexander Solzhenitsyn who wrote: 'The line separating good and evil passes not through states, not between classes, not between political parties . . . but right through every human heart and through all human hearts'. The cross is at once the darkest expression of evil and yet it is expression of God's ultimate victory in a dark world. The Good News happens when those initiated into heaven share with those to be met in mission the knowledge that evil and good are to be found together in one cross, in all our hearts. We are each a saint and a sinner. But if we embrace the cross and what it symbolizes the evil shall be transformed into good.

The second significance of stumbling-block, folly and Good News is that ultimately truth stands and prevails. The mighty ones and the wise ones could not believe the claims of Jesus. They even called him an imposter (Matt. 27.63), one who leads people astray. They did all to suppress the truth. But the experience of history is that truth stands. And so, in today's mission the task is to make known God's truth in a world of rival claims, in the face of the falsehood of idolatry and ideologies like the doctrine of national security, of dictatorships, of false belief systems.

Thirdly, the cross, symbolizing weakness and disgrace, and yet also symbolizing selfless and self-giving devotion to one another and humility, is the way to hope. Mission is an expression of the selfless and self-giving devotion to others. But that is more than charity; it is to build strategies of liberation in imitation of Christ who on the cross challenged all that did not conform to the will and plan of God. There is more to mission than just charity and development projects.

Lastly, the Good News of the cross is the language of faith. That is why Paul insists that the message is the power of salvation to those being saved and those who believe. Faith, when all around makes such belief folly, is to dream utopia. Such a dreaming stretches the mind to think of possibilities that by themselves dare not be thought. Better still, it is when the dreaming is done together with others that a new reality is born. That is the hope to which the folly of the cross invites us.

Mission to largely non-literate peoples: Appropriate communication

The South is a very complex area. On the one hand, we have those so educated in Northern culture and lifestyle that sometimes they seem to beat the northerners on their own home ground. But there are many more who have not been schooled in Northern arts. They are largely illiterate but not unintellectual. I draw attention to this to emphasize that we need a new language in order to communicate the message of the cross. In my encounter with illiterate people, I have experienced them to be sophisticated. With one proverb they confuse the so-called learned. The challenge in such evangelization is to communicate intelligently the word of the cross which is our hope.

One important area is appropriate symbolism. In a presentation to the 1988 Congress of the International Association for Mission Studies in Rome I wrote: 'Finite human beings thrive on symbols and indeed, appear unable to survive without symbols. And so it is that in the New Testament the cross is the symbol of hope of salvation. The cross is the symbol of Jesus dying to everything else, which fulfilled god-like possibilities like love, freedom, integrity, creativity and hope. But as humans, we do need other symbols to help us hold on to hope'.[10] The task is to find and develop such symbolism from within our Southern experience as will illumine the message of the folly and scandal of the cross which turns out to be Good News. In making this plea, people may warn me against the danger of idolatry or syncretism. But such fears have often been excuses for foreign dominance and captivity. Appropriate symbolism need not be idolatry or syncretism. Evangelism without regard for appropriate and local symbolism is doomed to failure. The Decade of Evangelism will yield dividends only if attention is paid to the use of appropriate local symbols to communicate. The cross itself is a symbol – the symbol of dying to everything else, which fulfilled god-like possibilities like love, freedom, integrity, creativity and therefore hope. Which symbolism will capture this among the predominantly non-literate peoples of Africa and elsewhere? That is the task of mission and of theology.

There is another aspect of appropriate communication – there is a need for new epistemology. Thanks to the Enlightenment, reflection on the faith tends to start with ideas as points of departure – often we start with a doctrine, a revelation, or reason on the assumption that all people perceive and articulate reality in the same way. We have learnt from liberation theology that it is more creative and convincing to start with social relations, in this case, 'the cry of the oppressed'. The dynamism of mission in the South derives in part from this new epistemology. Without a new epistemology, the folly and scandal of the cross cannot be reinterpreted to be Good News.

Not to give birth to Anglicans, but to bring people into God's household

This essay has been designed to serve the Decade of Evangelism declared by the Anglican Communion. Mercifully the contributors are not all

Anglicans. But I cannot help reflecting that other denominations have struck similar tones. The church exists for mission and, therefore, to be called to one's missionary vocation is very much in place. Mission however, is not to call people to be Anglicans or Roman Catholics or Presbyterians. The goal is to call people to realize themselves as real bodies or persons in God's household. Household is what the Greek word *oikos* means and from *oikos* we derive the word ecumenical. At the foot of the cross all are reconciled and peace is made (cf. Col. 1.20). The folly of the cross which we preach has to be prosecuted under an ecumenical perspective. My forbear, Philip Quaque, was so Anglican that he would have nothing to do with non-Anglicans. The Anglican Communion rightly calls us to be in mission. But the goal, if the cross is properly preached, is not to increase our numbers as Anglicans but to selflessly call all humanity to take their rightful place in God's household. We must not lose sight of the dominical saying: 'there are other sheep of mine, not belonging to this fold . . .' (John 10.16). God's family are not only Christians. While the cross may be our flag, we may never forget that others besides us are in God's household. This means, among other things, a sharing of initiatives and projects across the lines. It means that mission is dialogue with others, above all with the body and soul of Africans and their culture.[11]

Folly of mission by all and to all peoples

One last point – mission has often been in terms of movement from North to South. That was one expression of the folly of the cross. Under the impulse of the cross, people left the relative comfort of Europe to go to disease-infested Africa – Albert Schweitzer, medical doctor, theologian, musician and philosopher left a brilliant career to do less lucrative mission work in the jungles of Africa. For many his head needed examining. But his work has been the Good News of the cross.

Today, however, we need to think of mission in terms of mission on all continents, a phrase from the 1963 Mexico World Conference on Mission. All are missionaries and all are recipients of mission. That change demands of us that we dare to be foolish enough to believe that the so-called 'benighted Africans' have the capacity to be missionaries to themselves and to others. My predecessor in the chair of theology at the University of Ghana tells me a lovely story which illustrates the point. He was a student in Basel during the World War. He and a cousin went into a restaurant for a meal. The waiter took an interest in them and embarked on a conversation with them. Then came the point where the waiter asked their names. Prof. Baeta, my predecessor, responded 'Christian Baeta'. Thereupon the Swiss waiter burst into laughter and said: 'Christian? Is that a boast or an aspiration?' He could not believe that there could be Christians in Africa, even though Basel Mission had been at work in Ghana since the 19th century. He would not believe that God had been gathering Africans into his household for some time. And he could less have believed that Baeta was being prepared to lead the Evangelical Presbyterian Church of the Gold Coast, whose Synod Clerk he became. This story can be multiplied even in the contemporary behaviour of mission societies. Dare we believe that in God's inscrutable wisdom these Africans, children of European missionaries and churches in the faith, can be and are God's instruments and are called to be missionaries to themselves and to others. By human reckoning such thinking is folly; it is scandalous. But there is ample evidence that these nothings had been God's bearers of the Good News. Blessed be God who shares Good News through that which by the standards of the world is stumbling block and folly.

Notes

1 Barrett, 'AD2000: 350 million Christians in Africa' in *International review of mission* (59/ 1970, pp 39-54); A. F. Walls, 'Africa's place in Christian history' in J. S. Pobee (ed) *Religion in a pluralistic society* (E. J. Brill, Leiden, 1976, pp 180-189); R. D. Winter, *The twenty unbelievable years 1945-1969* (South Pasadena, 1978).
2 J. S. Pobee, *Persecution and martyrdom in the theology of Paul* (Academic Press, Sheffield, 1985).
3 E. Stählin, *Skandalon* in *Theological dictionary of the New Testament*, Volume 7, 1971 (Wm. B. Eerdmann, Grand Rapids, 1971, pp 352-356).
4 F. Bertram, *Moros et al* in *Theological dictionary of the New Testament*, Volume 4, 1967 (Ibid).
5 John de Gruchy, *Cry justice* (Collins, London, 1986, pp 36-38); Rebecca de Saintonge, *Outside the gate* (Spire, London, 1989).
6 M. M. Thomas, *Toward a contemporary theology of contemporary ecumenism* (Christian Literary Society, Madras/World Council of Churches, Geneva, 1978, p 181).
7 James R. Brockman, *Romero: A Life* (Orbis, New York, 1989, pp 83-84).
8 Ibid p 161.
9 J. S. Pobee, 'I am first an African and second a Christian' in *Indian missiological review* (Volume 10, No. 3, July 1989, pp 268-277).
10 J. S. Pobee, 'Hoping against hope? A biblical perspective' in *Mission studies: Journal of the international association for mission studies* (10, Volume 5, part 2, 1988, p 52).
11 J. S. Pobee, U. Schoen and J. P. Rajashekar (eds), *Encounter of religions in African cultures* (LWF, Geneva, 1991).

Notes on Contributors

Dr R. S. Sugirtharajah is Lecturer in Third World Theologies at the Department of Mission, Selly Oak, UK. His areas of personal research and interest include biblical hermeneutics, multi-faith hermeneutics and Third World theologies. His publications include *Voices from the margin: Interpreting the Bible in the Third World* (SPCK, London, 1991).

Musimbi Kanyoro is Kenyan. She has worked in many countries of Africa in the field of Bible translations as a consultant for the United Bible Society. She is currently working in Geneva with the Lutheran World Federation.

Reinhild Traitler is Director of women's work with the Evangelical Academy, Bolden, Switzerland. She has had extensive ecumenical experience and has worked in liberation theology. She is the author of many publications both in German and in English.

Kosuke Koyama is Professor of Ecumenics and World Christianity at Union Theological Seminary, New York, USA. He is an ordained minister of the Church of Christ in Thailand. His publications include *Mt Fuji and Mt Sinaii* (SCM Press, London, 1984).

Rev. Raquel Rodriguez is from Puerto Rico. Recently ordained as a Lutheran pastor, she lives in Costa Rica where she works as a researcher in the Department of Ecumenical Research. She focuses on women's struggles and publishes materials from a Latin American ideological perspective.

Fr Albert Nolan, a Roman Catholic priest from South Africa, is on the staff of the Institute for Contextual Theology in Johannesburg and is the author of several books, including *Jesus before Christianity* and *God in South Africa*.

K. H. Ting, an Anglican bishop, is Principal of Nanjing Theological College, and Vice-President and Head of Religious Studies at Nanjing University.

Fr Tissa Balasuriya, OMI is the Director of the Centre for Society and Religion in Colombo, Sri Lanka. He has travelled extensively in Europe, the United States and Asia conducting workshops and seminars. His publications include *Eucharist and human liberation* (Orbis, New York, 1977) and *Planetary theology* (Orbis, New York, 1984).

John S. Pobee is an Anglican and a Ghanaian. He has taught New Testament and Missiology in universities in Europe and Africa and is the President of the International Association for Mission Studies. His publications include *Towards an African theology* (Abingdon, Nashville, 1979), *Mission in Christ's way* (ISPCK, New Delhi, 1989) and *Who are the poor?* (WCC, Geneva, 1987). He is currently on leave of absence from the University of Ghana where he has been Professor and head of the Department for the Study of Religions and Dean of the Faculty of Arts, to serve as Associate Director of the Programme on Ecumenical Theological Education – Bossey. He has been Vice-President of the International Association for Mission Studies (IAMS) and has been President since 1988.